INTRODUCTION TO SYNCHRONIZED SWIMMING

Jean Lundholm

University of Wisconsin
Madison, Wisconsin

Mary Jo Ruggieri

Ohio State University
Columbus, Ohio

Illustrated by

Barbara Sanborn Jones

Burgess Publishing Company
Minneapolis, Minnesota

Consulting Editors to the Publisher

Eloise M. Jaeger
    University of Minnesota
    Minneapolis, Minnesota

Robert M. Clayton
    Colorado State University
    Fort Collins, Colorado

Copyright © 1976 by Burgess Publishing Company
Printed in the United States of America
Library of Congress Catalog Card Number 75-44632
ISBN 0-8087-1232-2

All rights reserved. No part of this book may be reproduced in any form whatsoever, by photograph or mimeograph or by any other means, by broadcast or transmission, by translation into any kind of language, nor by recording electronically or otherwise, without permission in writing from the publisher, except by a reviewer, who may quote brief passages in critical articles and reviews.

10 9 8 7 6 5 4 3 2 1

Dedicated to our parents, for without their encouragement and support the writing of this book would not have been possible.

5 2 5 68

CONTENTS

PREFACE

Synchronized swimming is composed of basic body positions, swimming strokes and stroke variations, sculls for propulsion and support, and figures and hybrid figures. The first chapter of *Introduction to Synchronized Swimming* presents the reader with a background in movement principles. Following this chapter, detailed explanations of basic body positions, strokes and stroke variations, and sculls for propulsion and support are provided.

Once the strokes and sculls are discussed the emphasis is directed toward teaching basic movements. The Amateur Athletic Union publishes a synchronized swimming handbook that lists approximately 135 figures. Each figure is classified, described, and given a degree of difficulty. This handbook is often used by teachers of synchronized swimming. Because of the vast number of figures listed it becomes extremely frustrating if one attempts to teach a figure by reading the step-by-step description. It is also difficult to determine what figure should be taught first and which ones should follow.

A simple solution to the problem of teaching figures is the use of movement progressions. These progressions are combinations of body positions, component parts of figures, and related movements which are listed in sequential order and which start from the simple and move to the complex. As the swimmer moves through these progressions she becomes kinesthetically aware of her movement capabilities. She can then systematically progress to the more difficult tasks.

Approximately seventy progressions have been defined by the authors and placed into one of seven general categories. The purpose of the progressions is to provide workable formats for learning or teaching which can be used by any individual. *Every figure listed in the rule book is simply a combination of one or more of the movement progressions.*

In addition to learning figures, synchronized swimmers must engage in properly organized dry-land and water exercise programs in order to attain and maintain the level of strength, flexibility, and endurance which is necessary for successful participation in the sport. Numerous training and conditioning methods are discussed and various dry-land exercises and water drills are described.

Upon mastery of the fundamentals of synchronized swimming, the swimmer can organize and combine these skills in a routine or composition. The way in which these skills are combined will be dependent upon the type of organization in which the swimmer wishes to participate. Therefore, brief descriptions of the Amateur Athletic Union, International Academy of Aquatic Art, and intercollegiate organizations are provided in Chapter 15. Basic principles of choreography to aid the novice in routine development are explained in Chapter 16.

It is quite likely that the teacher or coach will be called upon to host competitive synchronized swimming meets. Chapter 17 gives the coach a workable format to follow when hosting such meets.

In summarizing the material, a detailed unit plan has been provided. The instructor or coach should find it helpful in organizing the basic curriculum of skill development applicable to her type of program.

There are other aspects of synchronized swimming, such as show production and judging. It would be difficult to cover all areas sufficiently in one book. Therefore, *Introduction to Synchronized Swimming* is designed to provide only that material which is necessary for the development of any successful program.

This book could not have been written without the help of many individuals. We would like to thank all of our synchronized swimmers who were willing to try our movement progressions and training ideas. Years of teaching with the progressions and training concepts have helped us in developing all levels of synchronized swimmers and in coaching our synchronized swimming teams.

Sincere appreciation is extended to Myrtle Heid for editing, to Mrs. Richard Whelan for indexing, to Julia Brown and Bonita Hulbert for critically reviewing the material, and to Mary Raysa for assisting with the typing and editing. A special thanks is extended to Phyllis J. Bailey for her continued support in the development of synchronized swimming at the college level.

Jean Lundholm
Mary Jo Ruggieri

Chapter 1

CONCEPTS RELATED TO SYNCHRONIZED SWIMMING

A beginning synchronized swimmer often attains a high level of performance by engaging in a process of trial and error learning. If one is fortunate enough to choose the correct response, success will be achieved. Without really understanding why a particular movement accomplishes a desired result, the swimmer may randomly pick and choose until she eventually finds success.

If the swimmer has an understanding of the fundamental tenets of movement related to synchronized swimming, efficiency in learning will be increased. For this reason, the following concepts are offered. Much of this material is oversimplified to aid the reader in understanding these basic concepts. Exaggerated locations of the centers of gravity and buoyancy are offered to give the reader an idea of how these centers influence performance.

CONCEPTS OF STABILITY
ARCHIMEDES' PRINCIPLE OF BUOYANCY

Archimedes' principle of buoyancy states that any object immersed in a liquid is buoyed up by a force equal to the weight of the liquid that it displaces. Water, therefore, exerts a lifting force on an immersed body.

The mass of a swimmer or the weight per unit volume is called density and is related to the concept of buoyancy. Because of density, a small girl who has a high density factor may have difficulty floating. Density

is affected by the composition of the body. For example, bone and muscle weigh more per unit volume than adipose tissue or fat and are, therefore, denser.

Relative density is explained by using the term specific gravity—the ratio of the weight or mass of the body to an equal volume of water. The specific gravity of water is given at 1.0. If the weight or mass, per unit volume, of a swimmer is more than the specific gravity of water, the swimmer will sink. If a swimmer's weight or mass, per unit volume, is less than the specific gravity of water, she will float. Neutral buoyancy is obtained when the swimmer's specific gravity is equal to that of water.

Every swimmer has a distribution of body mass which determines her floating level. If she wishes to attain a higher floating level, she can increase the amount of air taken into the lungs. This decreases her specific gravity by increasing the volume of water displaced.

CENTER OF GRAVITY

The center of gravity is an imaginary point about which the weight of an object is equally distributed. The center of gravity of a human is usually located somewhere in the pelvic region (Figure 1-1). Individual differences in body build cause the location of this point to vary. A person with very broad shoulders and slender hips would have a center of gravity located slightly higher than average (Figure 1-2). Similarly,

1

Figure 1-1   Figure 1-2   Figure 1-3

Figure 1-4   Figure 1-5

a person with narrow shoulders and extremely muscular hips and thighs would have a center of gravity located slightly lower than average (Figure 1-3).

Each time a body part moves, the location of the center of gravity shifts in the direction of the movement. If the arms are raised above the head, the center of gravity moves in this direction, upward (Figure 1-4). If the arms are moved to one side, the center of gravity also moves to that side (Figure 1-5).

When a synchronized swimmer of average body build is in a layout, back, position, the center of gravity is located somewhere in the pelvic region (Figure 1-6). If the knee and hip joints are flexed to execute a ballet-leg, the body parts will move slightly upward and toward the head. The center of gravity then shifts toward the indicated direction (Figure 1-7). As the knee extends to the ballet-leg position, the center of gravity continues to shift in these directions (Figure 1-8).

CENTER OF BUOYANCY

The center of buoyancy is an imaginary point which represents the center of gravity of the displaced fluid of a floating object. It is usually located in the thorax area of the human. The location of this point is dependent upon lung capacity and body

Figure 1-6

Figure 1-7

Figure 1-8

composition. A swimmer with fatty hips and thighs would have a center of buoyancy somewhat lower than average. Similarly, a person with a greater lung capacity and slim thighs and legs would have a center of buoyancy somewhat higher than average.

STATIC EQUILIBRIUM IN THE WATER

A human floats motionless when his center of buoyancy and his center of gravity fall in the same vertical line of gravity. This line of gravity is an imaginary vertical line which passes through the center of gravity. When immersed in water, the body will rotate about the center of buoyancy until this condition is met (Figures 1-9, 1-10).

Figure 1-9

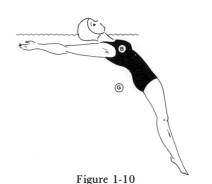

Figure 1-10

Rotation to a position of static equilibrium is an automatic response and is often observed when a beginning synchronized swimmer attempts to perform a ballet-leg, single, and fails to provide enough force by sculling (see Chapter 4). As the ballet-leg is lifted, instead of being kept perpendicular to the surface of the water, it is over-extended toward the face. This causes the center of gravity to shift in the same direction, toward the face and closer to the center of buoyancy (Figures 1-11, 1-12). At the same time, the knee of the leg on the surface of the water flexes and the hip hyperextends, causing the center of gravity to move closer to the same line of gravity as the center of buoyancy (Figure 1-13). This is usually the point at which the beginner gives up.

Figure 1-11

Figure 1-12

Figure 1-13

APPLICATION OF THE CONCEPTS OF STABILITY

The synchronized swimmer need not be concerned with memorizing the definitions of buoyancy, center of gravity, center of buoyancy, or static equilibrium, for apart from each other they are of little value. Instead, practical application of these concepts must be made each time she attempts to maintain a body position. The following analysis should aid the swimmer in understanding how these concepts apply to synchronized swimming.

Layout, Back

When a synchronized swimmer of average body build assumes a layout, back, the approximate center of gravity is in the pelvic region. Unless a force is applied, the body will automatically assume a position of static equilibrium. The center of gravity will drop directly beneath the center of buoyancy until it falls into the same line of gravity. Thus, the hips and legs will rotate toward the bottom. To prevent the body from rotating, the swimmer must apply force close to the center of gravity and toward the bottom of the pool (Figure 1-14).

Figure 1-14

Inverted Vertical

When a synchronized swimmer of average body build assumes an inverted vertical, the approximate locations of the center of gravity and center of buoyancy are in the same regions as in the layout, back. Because the center of gravity and center of buoyancy are in the same line of gravity, when the waterline is at the ankles the swimmer needs to apply only enough force to keep the body in line (Figure 1-15).

Crane

When a synchronized swimmer of average body build assumes a crane position, the approximate location of the center of buoyancy is in the chest area. As was previously stated, each time a body part moves, the location of the center of gravity shifts in the direction of the movement. In

Figure 1-15

the crane position, one leg is flexed 90 degrees at the hip, which means a body part has moved away from the midline of the body and toward the head. Thus, the center of gravity has shifted in the same direction. Once again, unless a force is applied close to the center of gravity, the body will rotate to a position of static equilibrium (Figure 1-16).

From the discussion of the concepts of stability related to synchronized swimming, the following guidelines apply to maintaining body positions.

Figure 1-16

Before Attempting the Position

1. Determine floating ability of swimmer.
2. Determine approximate location of center of gravity.
3. Determine approximate location of center of buoyancy.

Maintaining the Position

1. Determine if a body part has shifted and, if so, in what direction.
2. Determine the new location of the center of gravity for the position, and the direction and amount of force required to prevent the body from rotating to a position of static equilibrium.

CONCEPTS OF MOTION

NEWTON'S LAW OF INERTIA

A body remains at rest or in uniform motion in a straight line unless it is acted upon by some external force. Thus, if a swimmer is in a position of static equilibrium, she will remain in that static position unless some external force such as sculling (see Chapter 4) is applied. Once the swimmer applies force and begins to move along the surface of the water, she will continue to move in the same direction at the same speed until acted upon by some external force, such as gravity or water resistance.

NEWTON'S LAW OF ACCELERATION

The change of speed of an object is directly proportional to the amount of force which is applied (the greater the force, the greater the change of speed). If the same amount of force is applied to two objects, the change of speed is directly proportional to the mass (the greater the mass, the less the change of speed). Thus, if swimmers with identical body builds are in positions of static equilibrium, the swimmer who is able to apply the greatest amount of force by sculling will travel at the greatest speed. Similarly, if swimmers of varying body builds are in positions of

static equilibrium, and each applies the same amount of force by sculling, the swimmer with the smallest body build will travel at the greatest speed.

This concept also applies to the relative amount of force required to lift or sustain a body part out of the water. In the following two examples the least amount of body mass is lifted when moving from a pike to a crane and therefore the least amount of force by sculling is needed (Figures 1-17, 1-18). In moving from a pike to a vertical a greater amount of body mass is lifted and therefore a greater amount of force by sculling is needed (Figures 1-19, 1-20).

Following are three examples of sustaining a body part out of the water: a layout, back, a ballet-leg, and the ballet-legs, double. The least amount of body mass is

Figure 1-17

Figure 1-18

Figure 1-19

Figure 1-21

Figure 1-20

Figure 1-22

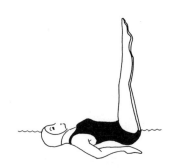

Figure 1-23

out of the water in the layout, back, and therefore the least amount of sculling force is needed (Figure 1-21). A greater amount of body mass is out of the water in the ballet-leg (Figure 1-22); the greatest amount of mass is out of the water in the ballet-legs, double (Figure 1-23), and therefore the greatest amount of sculling is needed.

NEWTON'S LAW OF ACTION AND REACTION

For every action there is an equal and opposite reaction. If a swimmer wishes to move headfirst, she must apply force in the opposite direction, toward the feet. If she wishes to move to the right, she must apply force to the left.

This concept becomes particularly evident when one observes the important role the head plays in determining the body position. If a swimmer in an inverted vertical position tucks her chin, the equal and opposite reaction that occurs is one of the following: she either falls on her back (Figures 1-24, 1-25) or flexes at the hips (Figures 1-26, 1-27). If she throws her head back, she will either fall on her face (Figures 1-28, 1-29) or arch her back (Figures 1-30, 1-31). In a layout, back, position, if the swimmer tucks her chin, either her legs will drop (Figures 1-32, 1-33) or her hips will flex (Figures 1-34, 1-35). Throwing the head back will cause the back to arch and the feet to sink (Figures 1-36, 1-37).

Figure 1-24

Figure 1-25

Figure 1-30

Figure 1-31

Figure 1-32

Figure 1-26

Figure 1-27

Figure 1-33

Figure 1-34

Figure 1-28

Figure 1-29

Figure 1-35

Figure 1-36

Figure 1-38

Figure 1-37

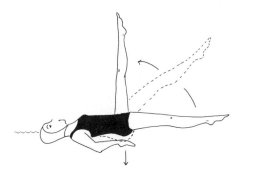

Figure 1-39

This concept is also obvious when one observes a synchronized swimmer lifting a body part out of the water. When a swimmer lifts a ballet-leg upward from a layout, back, position, the equal and opposite reaction that follows is a sinking of the hips (Figures 1-38, 1-39). When a swimmer lifts both legs upward to a vertical from a front pike position, the equal and opposite reaction that occurs is a submerging of the entire body (Figures 1-40, 1-41).

RESISTANCE AND PROPULSION

The two forces which act upon the body when it moves through the water are resistance and propulsion. Resistance is the force which retards the movement, and propulsion is the force which moves the body in a desired direction. An understanding of both is important for successful performance in synchronized swimming.

Figure 1-40

Resistance

There are three types of resistance which affect the performance of movement in the water: frontal, skin, and eddy resistance. Only frontal resistance will be discussed, for it is the one of most concern to synchronized swimmers.

Frontal resistance is the force created by some surface area of the body which operates in the direction opposite to desired movement. If a swimmer is moving head-

Figure 1-41

first in a layout, back, position, the frontal resistance is the force of water against her head, shoulders, and forearms (Figure 1-42).

The amount of frontal resistance which occurs during movement in the water can be altered by changing the position of the body. The greater the surface area of the body that pushes against the water, the greater the amount of frontal resistance. Thus, if a swimmer is moving headfirst in a layout, back, and tucks her chin and flexes her hips, more surface area of the body will push against the water and more frontal resistance will occur (Figure 1-43). If the head is pulled in line and the body is streamlined, there will be less surface area of the body pushing against the water and, therefore, less frontal resistance (Figure 1-44).

Figure 1-42

Figure 1-43

Figure 1-44

Propulsion

Propulsion is the force which moves the body in a desired direction. Because of the law of action and reaction, the swimmer must direct this force opposite to that of desired motion. The amount of force or propulsion she creates can be altered by changing the amount of surface area that directs the force. A large amount of surface area creates more force than a small amount of surface area. For instance, if a swimmer is in a layout, back, and attempts to scull with her hands alone, there is only a small surface area to direct the force. If she uses her forearms as well, there is a much greater amount of surface area and much more force is created.

The application of force or propulsion should be as even as possible so that movement in the desired direction is efficient. In a layout, back, once the body is set in motion and overcomes inertia, a swimmer can achieve a relatively even application of force by sculling. Because the force is even, the body moves smoothly along the surface of the water.

The swimmer can also move the body by a method called finning. Unlike sculling, this method has a power and recovery phase. The hands and forearms produce force toward the feet during the power phase and then recover to the original position to exert power again. This action produces a series of jerks or starts and stops; thus, the swimmer uses some of her power to overcome inertia.

THEORETICAL SQUARE LAW

The amount of propulsion and resistance can be altered by changing the speed of movement. Each time a swimmer increases her speed, the amount of increase in propulsion and resistance which results is squared.

If a swimmer is supporting a ballet-leg, single, and wants to support ballet-legs, double, she can double her speed of sculling and create four times as much power as well as four times as much resistance. This action causes a greater loss of energy, however, because each time the speed of a muscle contraction is doubled, the energy expenditure of that muscle is cubed. Therefore, by doubling her speed of sculling, she applies four times as much force but uses eight times as much energy. Each swimmer must, therefore, determine how much force is needed to achieve maximum performance with minimum energy expenditure.

SELECTED REFERENCES

Broer, Marion R. *Efficiency of Human Movement.* 3rd ed. Philadelphia: W. B. Saunders Company, 1973.

Councilman, James E. *The Science of Swimming.* Englewood Cliffs, N.J.: Prentice-Hall, Inc., 1968.

Midlying, Joanna. *Swimming.* Philadelphia: W. B. Saunders Company, 1974.

O'Connell, Alice L., and Gardner, Elizabeth B. *Understanding the Scientific Basis of Human Movement.* Baltimore: The Williams & Wilkins Company, 1972.

Rackham, George. *Synchronized Swimming.* London: Faber and Faber, 1968.

Wells, Katherine. *Kinesiology: The Scientific Basis of Human Motion.* Philadelphia: W. B. Saunders Company, 1971.

Chapter 2

BODY POSITIONS

Synchronized swimming figures are simply combinations of movement transitions from one basic body position to another; therefore, one must be familiar with the specified body positions.

The purpose of this chapter is to provide an accurate description of each position and to diagram the *approximate* location of the center of buoyancy (B) and the center of gravity (G) for each position. After reviewing the principles of stability offered in the previous chapter, the reader should be able to predict the approximate location in which it is necessary to apply force in each position to prevent the body from rotating to a position of static equilibrium.

The location of these points is not completely accurate and is offered only to give the reader an idea of how the center of gravity shifts in various positions. For complete accuracy, a segmental analysis of the locations would be required.

The positions have been subdivided into those occurring in either the horizontal or vertical planes. Each body position is then classified as a layout, pike, or tuck position. If the spine is extended or hyperextended, and the hip and knee joints are extended, the position is classified as a layout. If the spine is extended, one or both hip joints are flexed, and the knees are extended, the position is classified as a pike. If the spine is flexed, and the hip and knee joints are flexed, the position is classified as a tuck.

HORIZONTAL PLANE

LAYOUT

Layout, Front The body is in a prone position. The ears, shoulders, hips, knees, ankles, and feet are in line and parallel to the surface of the water. The spine, ankles, and feet are extended (Figure 2-1).

Layout, Back The body is in a layout, back, position. The ears, shoulders, hips, knees, ankles, and feet are in line and parallel to the surface of the water. The spine, ankles, and feet are extended (Figure 2-2).

Figure 2-1

Figure 2-2

PIKE

Bent-Knee Variant, Front The body is in a prone position. The spine is extended and the ears, shoulders, hips, and the knee and ankle of one leg are in line and parallel to the surface of the water. The other leg is flexed at the hip and knee joints with the

11

toes contacting the medial portion of the extended leg as close to the buttocks as possible. The foot of the flexed leg must be at or above the knee. The ankles and feet are extended (Figure 2-3).

Figure 2-3

Bent-Knee Variant, Back The body is in a layout, back, position. The spine is extended and the ears, shoulders, hips, and the knee and ankle of one leg are in line and parallel to the surface of the water. The other leg is flexed at the hip and knee joints with the toes contacting the medial portion of the extended leg as close to the buttocks as possible. The foot of the flexed leg must be at or above the knee. The hip and knee of the flexed leg are in line and perpendicular to the surface of the water. The ankles and feet are extended (Figure 2-4).

Figure 2-4

Ballet-Leg, Single The body is in a layout, back, position. The ears, shoulders, hips, and the knee, ankle, and foot of one leg are in line and parallel to the surface of the water. The other leg is flexed 90 degrees at the hip, extended at the knee, and perpendicular to the surface of the water. The spine, ankles, and feet are extended (Figure 2-5).

Figure 2-5

T Position The body is in a prone position. The ears, shoulders, hips, and the knee, ankle, and foot of one leg are in line and parallel to the surface of the water. The other leg is flexed 90 degrees at the hip, extended at the knee, and perpendicular to the surface of the water, with the toes pointing toward the bottom of the pool. The spine, ankles, and feet are extended (Figure 2-6).

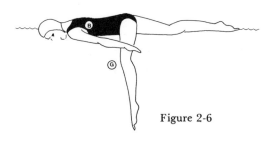

Figure 2-6

Flamingo The body is in a layout, back, position. The spine is extended and the ears, shoulders, and hips are in line and as close to parallel to the surface of the water as possible. One leg is flexed 90 degrees at the hip, extended at the knee, and perpendicular to the surface of the water. The other leg is flexed at the hip and knee joints with the midcalf contacting the medial portion of the extended leg. The knee and ankle of the flexed leg are in line

Figure 2-7

and parallel to the surface of the water. The ankles and feet are extended (Figure 2-7).

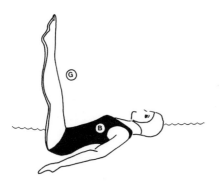

Figure 2-8

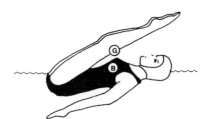

Figure 2-9

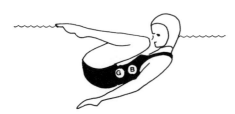

Figure 2-10

Ballet-Legs, Double The body is in a layout, back, position. The ears, shoulders, and hips are in line and as close to parallel to the surface of the water as possible. The legs are flexed 90 degrees at the hips so that the hips, knees, ankles, and feet are in line and perpendicular to the surface of the water. The ankles and feet are extended (Figure 2-8).

Back Pike The legs are flexed at the hips at as small an angle as possible. The hips, knees, ankles, and feet are in line, as are the ears, shoulders, and hips. The ankles and feet are extended (Figure 2-9).

TUCK

Surface Tuck The spine, hips, and knees are flexed and the ankles and feet are extended (Figure 2-10).

VERTICAL PLANE

LAYOUT

Inverted Vertical The head is toward the bottom of the pool. The ears, shoulders, hips, knees, ankles, and feet are in line and perpendicular to the surface of the water. The spine, ankles, and feet are extended (Figure 2-11).

Split The head is toward the bottom of the pool. The spine is hyperextended and the ears, shoulders, and hips are in line and perpendicular to the surface of the water. One leg is flexed and one leg is hyperextended so that the hip, knee, ankle, and foot of each leg are in line and parallel to the surface of the water. The ankles and feet are extended (Figure 2-12).

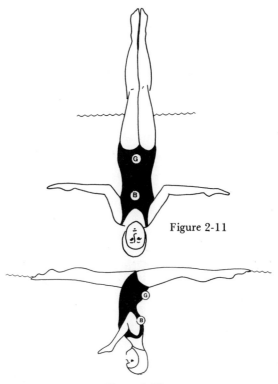

Figure 2-11

Figure 2-12

Knight The head is toward the bottom of the pool. The spine is hyperextended and the ears, shoulders, hips, and the knee, ankle, and foot of one leg are in line and perpendicular to the surface of the water. The other leg is hyperextended so that the knee, ankle, and foot are in line and parallel to the surface of the water. The ankles and feet are extended (Figure 2-13).

PIKE

Bent-Knee Variant The head is toward the bottom of the pool. The ears, shoulders, hips, and the knee, ankle, and foot of one leg are in line and perpendicular to the surface of the water. The other leg is flexed at the hip and knee joints with the toes contacting the medial portion of the extended leg as close to the buttocks as possible. The foot of the flexed leg must be at or above the knee. The spine, ankles, and feet are extended (Figure 2-14).

Crane The head is toward the bottom of the pool. The ears, shoulders, hips, and the knee, ankle, and foot of one leg are in line and perpendicular to the surface of the water. The other leg is flexed 90 degress at the hip, extended at the knee, and parallel to the surface of the water. The spine, ankles, and feet are extended (Figure 2-15).

Figure 2-14

Figure 2-15

Figure 2-13

Front Pike The head is toward the bottom of the pool. The ears, shoulders, and hips are in line and perpendicular to the surface of the water. The legs are flexed 90 degrees at the hips so that the hips, knees, ankles, and feet are in line and parallel to the surface of the water. The ankles and feet are extended (Figure 2-16).

TUCK

Inverted Tuck The head is as close to the midline of the body as possible. The spine, hips, and knees are flexed and the ankles and feet are extended. The legs from the knees to the toes are perpendicular to the surface of the water (Figure 2-17).

Figure 2-16

Figure 2-17

Chapter 3

STROKES, STROKE VARIATIONS, AND EGGBEATER KICK

An area of vital importance to synchronized swimming is the development of sound stroke mechanics. Therefore, this chapter will provide general descriptions of six basic strokes, suggest stroke variations that can be used in synchronized swimming routines, and discuss the eggbeater kick.

STROKES

FRONT CRAWL (Figures 3-1, 3-2, 3-3)

Body Position

The body should be streamlined and riding as close to the surface of the water as possible. The waterline is established somewhere between the eyebrows and hairline, depending upon the buoyancy of the swimmer. A swimmer with buoyant hips and thighs would require a waterline close to the eyebrows so that the legs would remain beneath the surface and the balancing effect of the kick would occur under the water. A swimmer with bony or dense hips and thighs would require a water level closer to the hairline so that the legs would come closer to the surface and not create too much resistance or drag.

Arm Action

The arms work in opposition to each other: as one arm is in the power phase, the other arm is in the recovery phase. The thumb and index finger generally enter the water first, with the entry occurring direct-

ly in line with the shoulder. As the hand sinks slightly, the elbow extends and a catch is made by flexing the wrist. The elbow begins to flex as the palm of the hand and forearm press backward against

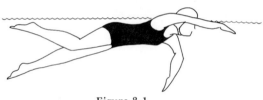

Figure 3-1

Figure 3-2

Figure 3-3

17

the water toward the midline of the body. The upper arm medially rotates to keep the elbow high. The elbow continues to flex to an approximate 90-degree angle. At this point the arm is directly under the body and halfway through the pull. A final push is made by extending the elbow and moving the palm toward the feet and the thumb toward the thigh.

A recovery is made by lifting the elbow high and relaxing the lower arm and hand. This recovery should be as close to the body as is comfortable for the swimmer, to prevent fishtailing or moving the feet from side to side.

Kick

The flutter kick is used with the front crawl and its major purpose is to stabilize and streamline the body. The legs work in opposition to each other: as one leg moves downward, it flexes at the hip and knee and then completely extends at the knee; the other leg moves upward with extended knee, by extending at the hip. The ankles remain loose and relaxed and the feet toe-in slightly. Most of the leg action is generated from the hip muscles; the down-beat of the kick gives most of the power.

Breathing

Inhalation usually occurs at the completion of the power phase of the arm on the breathing side. If breathing is timed correctly, the mouth will be turned into the bow wave during inhalation. After inhalation through the mouth, the face is turned into the water and exhalation through the mouth and nose continues until the next inhalation occurs.

Coordination

In the front crawl there is continuous movement with no pause in the arm stroke or flutter kick. Usually there are six flutter kicks to each complete arm cycle. Breathing usually occurs on the same side, once every arm cycle.

Throughout the stroke it is important for the body to roll from side to side. This guideline can be followed: first the right ear comes out of the water and then the left ear comes out, with the head in line with the body throughout the roll. This roll drops the shoulder of the power arm under the water for greater strength, facilitates breathing, and makes it easier for the arm to recover.

BACK CRAWL (Figures 3-4, 3-5, 3-6)

Body Position

The body should be streamlined and riding as close to the surface as possible. The ears should be in the water and the head should maintain a stationary position with little or no lateral movement.

Arm Action

The arms work in opposition to each other: as one arm is in the recovery phase, the other arm is in the power phase. The

Figure 3-4

Figure 3-5

Figure 3-6

little finger generally enters the water first, with the entry occurring directly in line with the shoulder. As the hand sinks slightly, a catch is made by flexing the wrist. When the hand is in line with the shoulder, the elbow begins to flex and the palm of the hand and forearm press against the water toward the feet. The upper arm begins to rotate medially to keep the elbow high. The elbow continues to flex to an approximate 90-degree angle. At this point the arm is midway between the shoulder and waist and halfway through the pull. A final press is made by continuing the medial rotation of the upper arm, extending the elbow, and moving the palm toward the feet and the thumb toward the thigh. The finished position of the hand is below the level of the hip with the palm toward the bottom. This flip initiates the body roll.

Kick

The flutter kick is used with the back crawl and its major purpose is to stabilize and streamline the body. The legs work in opposition to each other: as one leg moves upward, it flexes at the hip and knee and then completely extends at the knee; the other leg moves downward with extended knee, by extending at the hip. The ankles remain loose and relaxed and the feet toe-in slightly. Most of the leg action is generated from the hip muscles. The upbeat of the kick gives most of the power.

Breathing

Breathing is free, since the face is up. Sometimes it is good to establish a breathing pattern because it aids the rhythm of the stroke. Inhaling on one arm recovery and exhaling on the other can be used as a pattern.

Coordination

In the back crawl there is continuous movement with no pause in the arm stroke or flutter kick. Usually there are six flutter kicks to each complete arm cycle.

Throughout the stroke it is important for the body to roll from side to side with the head set. This roll drops the shoulder of the power arm under the water on the entry for greater strength on the first part of the pull. It also facilitates the recovery and prevents the hand of the power arm from coming out of the water.

BREASTSTROKE (Figures 3-7, 3-8, 3-9, 3-10)

Body Position

The body should be as streamlined as possible with the shoulders and hips riding close to the surface. The head position

Figure 3-7

Figure 3-8

Figure 3-9

Figure 3-10

should remain constant, with the waterline somewhere between the hairline and the eyebrows, depending upon the buoyancy of the swimmer. One important factor in the body position of the breaststroke is that the shoulders and hips should be held parallel to the surface of the water for less resistance.

Arm Action

The arms work simultaneously. At the start of the power phase the arms are fully extended and slightly below the surface of the water. A catch is made by flexing the wrists. The elbows begin to flex as the palms of the hands and forearms press down and back. The upper arms rotate medially to keep the elbows high. The elbows continue to flex to an approximate 90-degree angle and the hands remain inside the line of the shoulders throughout this pull. A final sculling action is made by laterally rotating the upper arms.

The recovery is made by bringing the elbows in close to the body and then extending the arms forward and slightly upward. The recovery should be made quickly in order to get the hands to a position where the next stroke can occur effectively.

Kick

The breaststroke kick is used and its major purpose is propulsion. The legs work simultaneously.

To begin the recovery, the hips and knees are flexed with the heels drawn tight to the buttocks and the knees slightly separated. The optimum angle of hip flexion is approximately 100 degrees. In preparation for the power phase the thighs are rotated medially and the ankles dorsiflexed. The insides of the ankles and the soles of the feet press backward in a slightly circular motion. The knees and ankles do not fully extend until the completion of the kick. A slight press up on the heels will help in returning to a stream-

lined body position. The power of the kick comes from the hip extensors.

Breathing

The inhalation occurs when the shoulders are at the highest point, generally just prior to the completion of the power phase of the arm action. At this point the chin is raised by hyperextending the neck (like butting a ball forward with the chin). The mouth should be in the bow wave and the chin on the surface of the water. After inhalation through the mouth, the face is lowered into the water and exhalation through the mouth and nose continues until the next inhalation occurs.

Coordination

The arms and legs alternate in propelling action. The power phase of the arm action begins and just prior to the recovery the head is lifted for a breath. As the inhalation occurs, the recovery of the kick begins. Just prior to the completion of the recovery of the arms the power phase of the legs begins. At the completion of the power phase of the legs a glide is held just long enough to use the forward momentum created.

BUTTERFLY (Figures 3-11, 3-12, 3-13, 3-14, 3-15)

Body Position

The body should be flat and as streamlined as possible, considering the nature of the undulating movements within the stroke. The head is held at a constant water level somewhere between the hairline and eyebrows. The shoulders and hips should remain parallel to the surface of the water.

Arm Action

The arm action is very similar to the front-crawl action. The arms work simultaneously with a double arm pull and a double arm recovery. Depending upon the swimmer, the pull is usually done in an "hourglass" design.

Figure 3-11

Figure 3-12

Figure 3-13

Figure 3-14

Figure 3-15

The thumb and index fingers generally enter the water first, with the entry occurring directly in line with the shoulders. As the hands sink slightly the elbows extend and a catch is made by flexing the wrists. There is a slight pull out as the elbows flex and the upper arms rotate medially to keep the elbows high. The elbows continue to flex and the upper arms rotate medially until the fingertips are almost touching. At this point the elbows are flexed approximately 90 degrees, the arms are directly under the body, and one half of the "hourglass" design is completed. A final push is made by extending the elbows and pressing the palms toward the feet and the thumbs toward the thighs.

A recovery is made by lifting the elbows and swinging the arms forward with the backs of the hands leading. When the arms are in line with the shoulders the arms are rotated laterally to facilitate proper entry.

Kick

The dolphin kick is used with the butterfly and its major purpose is propulsion and stabilization. The kick is similar to a flutter kick with the legs held together. As both legs move downward they flex at the hips and knees and then completely extend at the knees. This causes the hips to raise. Both legs then move upward with extended knees, by extending at the hips. This causes the hips to sink slightly. The ankles remain loose and relaxed and the feet toe in slightly. Most of the leg action is generated from the hip muscles.

Breathing

The inhalation occurs when the shoulders are at the highest point, generally just prior to the completion of the power phase of the arm action. At this point the neck is hyperextended to let the mouth clear the water but permitting the chin to stay on the surface. After inhalation through the mouth, the face is dropped into the water. Exhalation through the mouth and nose occurs just before the next breath. It is important to have the face in the water by the time the arms are in line with the shoulders on the recovery. It is common to breathe once every two arm cycles.

Coordination

Most swimmers use two dolphin kicks for every one arm cycle. The first kick, usually the larger one, is done as the arms enter the water. The second kick is usually done just prior to the start of the recovery of the arm action.

SIDESTROKE (Figures 3-16, 3-17, 3-18, 3-19)

Body Position

The body position should be as streamlined as possible with the body on its side. The swimmer's ears, shoulders, hips, and ankles are as close to the surface of the water as possible.

Arm Action

The bottom arm is extended overhead and in line with the body. At the start of the pull the swimmer changes the pitch of the hand by flexing the wrist. As the pull begins the arm is rotated medially to keep the elbow high. The elbow flexes as the forearm and palm continue to press toward the feet. The upper portion of the arm

adducts at the shoulder until the elbow points toward the bottom of the pool. The elbow then flexes and the thumb leads toward the shoulder for recovery. The forearm is pronated so that the palm is toward the bottom of the pool and the arm extends overhead.

The top arm is extended with the palm resting on the thigh. To start the recovery the elbow flexes and the thumb leads toward the shoulder. With the fingertips leading, the arm extends toward the bottom of the pool anywhere between the chin and hips. The forearm and hand press toward the feet.

Kick

The scissors kick is used with the sidestroke and its major purpose is propulsion. The knees and ankles are extended.

To begin the recovery the knees and hips are flexed until an imaginary line can be drawn through the hips, shoulders, and mid-calf. Throughout this flexion the ankles are extended. As the top leg reaches forward the ankle is flexed. At the same time the bottom leg reaches back with the ankle extended. The knees extend as the legs make a circular action. The knees are not fully extended until the completion of the kick.

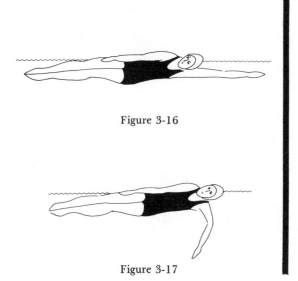

Figure 3-16

Figure 3-17

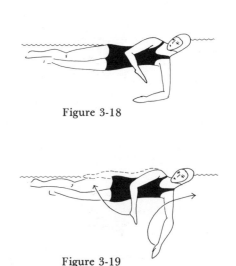

Figure 3-18

Figure 3-19

Breathing

Inhalation through the mouth occurs on the recovery of the top arm and legs. Exhalation through the mouth and nose occurs on the power phase of the top arm and the legs.

Coordination

The top arm and legs recover and propel together. The bottom arm works in opposition to the top arm. At the completion of the power phase of the legs a glide is held long enough to use the forward momentum created.

ELEMENTARY BACKSTROKE
(Figures 3-20, 3-21, 3-22, 3-23)

Body Position

The body should be streamlined and riding as close to the surface as possible. The ears should be in the water and the head should maintain a stationary position.

Arm Action

The arms are in an extended position with the palms at or near the thighs. The thumbs slide up the sides of the body while the elbows drop down toward the bottom of the pool. When the thumbs reach the armpits the forearms pronate and the arms

extend with the fingertips leading. The arms are extended to a position slightly above the level of the shoulders. The forearms and hands apply pressure toward the feet until they reach the extended position near the thighs.

Kick

The whip kick is used in the elementary backstroke and its major purpose is propulsion. The kick is the same as the breaststroke kick with the exception that there is not as much hip flexion.

Breathing

Breathing is free, since the face is up. Sometimes it is good to establish a breathing pattern because it aids the rhythm of the stroke. Inhaling on the recovery of the arms and exhaling on the power phase can be used as a pattern.

Coordination

The arms begin their recovery and when they are at or near the chest area the legs begin to recover. The important factor is that the power phases of the arms and legs finish together. At the completion of the power phase the glide is held long enough to use the forward momentum created.

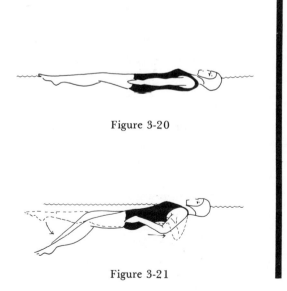

Figure 3-20

Figure 3-21

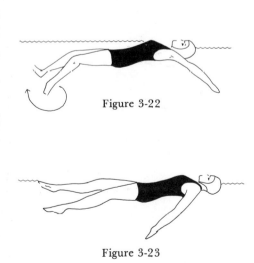

Figure 3-22

Figure 3-23

STROKE VARIATIONS

Any number of stroke combinations can be developed for use in synchronized swimming routines. These basic principles should be considered when synchronized swimming strokes are developed:

1. The swimmers should be able to perform the basic strokes correctly.

2. Arm strokes should stress out-of-the-water recoveries when possible.

3. Body positions should be held high and constant throughout the stroke. Bobbing up and down should be avoided.

4. Kicking action will be more vertical and slightly lower than in basic stroking.

5. Whenever possible, when one arm is not being used, a sculling action (see Chapter 4) should occur for more support.

6. The stroke should propel the swimmer in the water and/or be used for directional change.

7. Head changes can be added to all of the modified strokes.

The following are variations of the basic strokes.

MODIFIED FRONT CRAWL (Figure 3-24)

1. The head and shoulders are lifted out of the water and held in an upright position.

2. A straight arm or a bent arm can be used. The arm in the water sculls under the body for support.

Figure 3-24

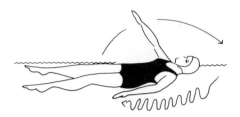

Figure 3-25

3. The kick is a regular front-crawl kick with more flexion at the knees. An egg-beater kick (see page 25) can also be used for more sustained height.

MODIFIED BACK CRAWL (Figure 3-25)

1. The emphasis is placed on sustaining the recovery of each arm stroke. The arm in the water sculls at or near the hip for support.

2. The kick is a regular back-crawl kick with more flexion at the knee.

MODIFIED SIDESTROKE

1. The head and shoulders are lifted out of the water.

2. A straight arm out-of-the-water recovery with the top arm can be used. The arm in the water sculls under the body for support.

3. The kick is a regular scissors kick.

MODIFIED BREASTSTROKE

1. The head and shoulders are lifted out of the water and held in an upright position.

2. The emphasis is placed on a shortened arm pull. Sculling, with both hands, under the body, should occur when possible.

3. The kick is a regular breaststroke kick with more flexion at the hips.

MODIFIED BUTTERFLY

1. Since the butterfly uses a double arm recovery, one or two arm strokes can be executed for emphasis in a routine.

2. The dolphin kick is a good propulsive technique and can be used either in a layout, front, position or a layout, side, position.

MODIFIED STROKE COMBINATIONS

1. A swish can be executed with a straight-arm freestyle stroke. The arm should be taken from behind the body to in front of the body with a rapid motion, swishing water as it moves.

2. Alternating a front crawl with a sidestroke is effective.

3. Performing a breaststroke and then rolling to a layout, side, for a sidestroke can be used.

4. Sidestroke to a forward swish to a breaststroke is another combination.

5. Quickly executing two backstrokes and then rolling to a layout, side, for a sidestroke movement is also effective.

Any number of modified stroke combinations can be developed. The tempo of the music, the desired directional change, and the amount of traveling needed in the routine are factors to consider before deciding upon the strokes to be used.

Figure 3-26

EGGBEATER KICK (Figures 3-26, 3-27)

The eggbeater kick is a propulsive and supportive technique used in synchronized swimming. It is used to support and give height to a swimmer in a vertical position. It is also used as a transitional kick to aid swimmers in going from one body position to another or in moving from one stroke transition to another.

The basic action of the kick is an alternating breaststroke kick with one foot moving clockwise and one foot moving counterclockwise. The back remains vertical and is perpendicular to the surface of the water. The hips are flexed to a 90-degree angle. The knees are spread far apart to give a large base of support.

Teaching Progressions

1. Breaststroke kick in a vertical position. Swimmers should use the hands to

Figure 3-27

scull for support and should thrust up on the power phase of the kick.

2. Have the swimmers hang on to the side of the pool with one arm and practice the kick with one leg. Change sides and alternate the practice leg.

3. Have the swimmers sit on the edge of a diving board and practice the kick.

4. "Eggbeater bobs"—have the swimmers drop toward the bottom of the pool and eggbeater up.

5. Start as soon as possible to incorporate the kick with stroke transitions.

Chapter 4

SCULLING

SCULLING FOR PROPULSION

Sculling for propulsion is basically a figure-eight motion with the forearms and hands moving first away from and then toward the body. The force created by this figure-eight sculling action must be directly opposite that of the desired movement.

An example of this would be in the stationary scull, layout, back, body position. The forearm and the hand sculling action will direct the force of the figure eight toward the bottom of the pool. This will result in no movement toward the head or the feet. In contrast, if the fingertips are lifted slightly so that the force of the figure eight is directed toward the feet, the body will move in the direction of the head.

When referring to sculling as a means of propulsion, the swimmer must always think in terms of application of force. Propulsion in sculling is that force which moves the body in the desired direction. Force must be applied in a direction opposite to that of the desired movement (Newton's Law of Action and Reaction). When teaching sculling, the instructor must emphasize the application of force.

The various hand and body positions that may be used in sculling for propulsion are as follows:

Sculls for Propulsion

Desired Direction	Body Position	Hand Position
1. Stationary Scull	Layout, Back	Hands at or near the hips
2. Stationary Scull	Layout, Front	Hands somewhere between the waist and the shoulders
3. Headfirst Scull	Layout, Back	Hands at or near the hips
4. Feetfirst Scull	Layout, Back	Hands at or near the hips
5. Headfirst Scull	Layout, Back	Hands overhead
6. Feetfirst Scull	Layout, Back	Hands overhead
7. Headfirst Scull	Layout, Front	Hands overhead
8. Feetfirst Scull	Layout, Front	Hands overhead
9. Feetfirst Scull	Layout, Front	Hands somewhere between the waist and the hips
10. Side Scull	Layout, Side	One hand used somewhere in the chest area

Swimmers can benefit from a logical teaching progression and frequent review of the basic sculls for propulsion. Descriptive terminology is preferable to nondescriptive names such as lobster scull or canoe scull. Swimmers will develop skills faster as a result of the understanding gained through the use of clear terminology. To teach the ten basic sculls, describe them in terms of body position, desired direction of movement, placement of the hands (this will vary slightly depending upon the swimmer's center of gravity and center of buoyancy), and sculling technique. The concept to be emphasized is that there are basic positions in which the sculling action does not change, and if these positions are learned, they can be transferred to all of the movement progressions.

SCULLING TECHNIQUES

1.   Stationary   Scull—Layout,   Back (Figure 4-1)

The hands are at or near the hips. The elbows flex to a 90-degree angle during the movement toward the body and extend during the movement away from the body. The hands and wrists describe figure-eight motions, with the palms of the hands remaining as flat as possible. The speed of the scull and the angle of the palms must be increased when more force is desired, as in lifting a ballet-leg, single.

Figure 4-1

2.   Stationary   Scull—Layout,   Front (Figure 4-2)

The hands are placed somewhere between the waist and the shoulders, depending upon the swimmer's center of gravity and center of buoyancy. The elbows flex to a 90-degree angle during the

movement toward the body and extend during the movement away from the body. The hands and wrists describe figure-eight motions, with the palms of the hands remaining as flat as possible. When the head is slightly lifted, it causes a corresponding arch in the back. The speed and range of the scull must, therefore, be increased.

Figure 4-2

3.   Headfirst   Scull—Layout,   Back (Figure 4-3)

The hands are placed at or near the hips. The elbows flex to approximately a 90-degree angle during the movement toward the body and extend during the movement away from the body. The fingertips are lifted slightly so that the figure-eight motion will be directed toward the feet.

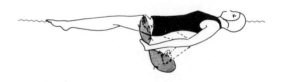

Figure 4-3

4.   Feetfirst   Scull—Layout,   Back (Figure 4-4)

The hands are placed at or near the hips. The wrists are flexed so that the thumbs and the fingertips are pointed toward the bottom. During the movement away from the body, the little fingers lead. The thumbs lead the movement inward. There is a continuous application of force toward the head during the scull.

Figure 4-4

5. Headfirst   Scull—Layout,   Back (Figure 4-5)

Both hands are extended overhead and the shoulders are relaxed in the water. The wrists are flexed so that the fingertips are pointed up toward the ceiling. The little fingers lead in the movement away from the body, and the thumbs lead the movement inward. There is a continuous application of force toward the feet during the scull.

Figure 4-5

6. Feetfirst   Scull—Layout,   Back (Figure 4-6)

Both hands are extended overhead and the shoulders are relaxed in the water. The palms of the hands are facing away from the feet. The little fingers are rotated away from the body and the thumbs rotate in. The elbows will flex slightly during the movement toward the body and will extend during the movement away from the body.

Figure 4-6

7. Headfirst   Scull—Layout,   Front (Figure 4-7)

This scull is often used as a primer for the pike down-front. It makes the swimmer aware of the direction in which force must be applied in order to obtain the forward motion needed in this body position. The hands are extended overhead, the wrists are flexed so that the fingertips point toward the bottom of the pool. The face can be in or out of the water. A figure-eight movement is described by having the little fingers leading the movement away from the body and the thumbs leading the movement in toward the body.

Figure 4-7

8. Feetfirst   Scull—Layout,   Front (Figure 4-8)

The hands are extended overhead, the wrists are hyperextended so that the fingertips point away from the bottom of the pool, and the face can be in or out of the water. The palms of the hands are facing away from the feet. The little fingers lead the movement away from the body, and the thumbs lead the movement in toward the body in a figure-eight action. The elbows will flex slightly during the movement toward the body and extend during the movement away from the body. A continuous application of force is needed opposite the desired direction.

Figure 4-8

9. *Feetfirst Scull—Layout, Front* (Figure 4-9)

The hand position for this scull may be somewhere between the waist and hip area, depending upon the swimmer's center of gravity and center of buoyancy. This scull is often used as a primer for teaching a sculling action for any swordfish type of movement progression. The elbows and wrists are flexed so that the palms face toward the head. During the movement away from the body, the thumbs of the hands lead. The little fingers lead the movement inward, thereby creating the desired figure-eight motion.

Figure 4-9

10. *Side Scull—Layout, Side* (Figure 4-10)

The body is in a layout, side, position. One arm is underwater while the non-propelling arm is either kept on the hip or the surface or held slightly in the air for balance. The sculling hand is directly under the body, palm facing slightly down and toward the feet. The elbow is flexed to a 90-degree angle. The thumb leads in toward the body and the little finger leads away from the body as the desired figure-eight action is obtained.

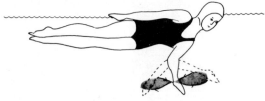

Figure 4-10

In all sculling techniques, good body positions are of utmost importance. Without the correct body position, the force created by the sculling may not be effective.

SCULLING FOR SUPPORT

Support sculling is a technique which supports the body by applying force toward the bottom of the pool. This movement is accomplished by flexing the elbow joints and catching the water with the forearms and hands as they move first away from and then toward the body in a plane relatively parallel to the surface of the water.

Teaching Progression (Figure 4-11)

To get the feel of the scull, the swimmer should assume an upright vertical position in the deep water so that the feet are toward the bottom of the pool. She should flex the elbows so that the palms are toward the surface as if holding a tray. By sweeping the forearms she should try to submerge to the bottom. The little fingers can touch on the in sweep.

Figure 4-11

INVERTED TUCK

Sculling Action

Because the center of gravity and center of buoyancy are close to the same line of gravity, only a slight amount of force is required to prevent rotation. The arms are almost fully extended with the elbows in close to the knees. The forearms and palms of the hands are toward the bottom of the pool and move in a nearly horizontal plane, first away from and then toward the midline of the body (Figure 4-12).

Figure 4-12

Teaching Progression

One swimmer assumes the tuck position in the shallow water with her arms extended and close to her knees. Her partner rolls her backward until her legs from the knees to the toes are perpendicular to the surface of the water (Figures 4-13, 4-14).

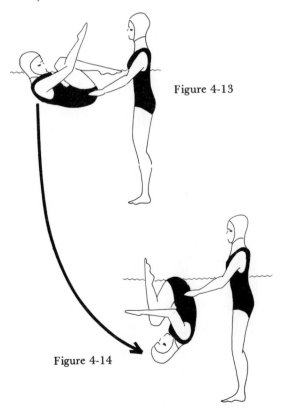

Figure 4-13

Figure 4-14

Checkpoint

From the pool deck, the observer should see the backs of the hands and not the palms. A swimmer who is not yet oriented to an inverted position will often flip the hands so that the palms are toward the surface. In this case, it helps if someone manually flips the hands back and moves them in the correct plane.

Common Errors

1. The elbows slip away from the knees, causing the body to roll completely around.

2. The elbows are flexed too tightly, causing the body to travel forward. Tell the swimmer to push her hands away from her face. Be sure to remind her that the elbows should be next to the sides of the knees and not under them.

3. Movement of the hands and forearms in a vertical rather than a relatively horizontal plane causes the body to travel backward or to tip over backward.

FRONT PIKE

Sculling Action

Because the center of gravity has shifted farther from the line of gravity than the center of buoyancy, a greater amount of force is required to prevent rotation than in the inverted tuck. The elbows are flexed and the backs of the hands are close to the knees. The forearms and palms of the hands are toward the bottom of the pool and move in a figure-eight pattern as they move first away and then toward the midline of the body (Figure 4-15).

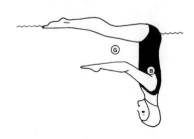

Figure 4-15

Teaching Progression

To provide the swimmer with the opportunity to practice the scull without working to hold the position, have a partner support her hips at the wall. Tell the swimmer to place the backs of her hands against her knees and begin again (Figure scull, and, in addition, when she gets confused, she can place the backs of her hands against her knees and being again (Figure 4-16). Hint: To maintain a pike, contract the abdominals and buttocks, extend the ankles and knees.

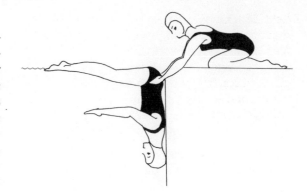

Figure 4-16

Common Errors

If the pike is less than 90-degrees and the shoulders are shoved forward, either the body will roll over or the feet will drop below the surface of the water.

BENT-KNEE VARIANT

Sculling Action

The sculling action is similar to the action in the front pike. Because the center of gravity is close to the center of buoyancy, the elbows are in closer, and the forearms and palms are out to the sides (Figure 4-17).

Figure 4-17

Teaching Progression

The swimmer can practice the sculling action against the wall while a partner supports the ankle of the vertical leg (Figure 4-18).

Common Errors

1. If the body tips toward the face, the swimmer should move her hands away from the midline of the body.

2. If the elbows are flexed less than 90 degrees, the swimmer will travel forward. The swimmer should push her hands away from her face.

SPLIT

Sculling Action

Because the center of gravity and center of buoyancy are close to the same vertical

Figure 4-18

line of gravity, very little force need be applied. The sculling action is accomplished by keeping the elbows in close to the waist and sweeping the forearms and palms out at the sides. The closer to the surface of the water, and greater the amount of stretch in the split, the higher the elevation (Figure 4-19).

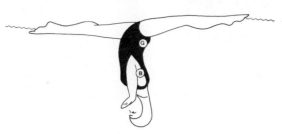

Figure 4-19

Teaching Progression

Before permitting the swimmer to scull, have her practice floating motionless in the split position. Check to see that her head is in line with her body and that both ankles are at the same water level.

Common Errors

1. The swimmer lifts one ankle off the surface of the water.
2. One leg is stretched more than the other, causing a rotation of the hips.

CRANE

Sculling Action

The sculling action for the crane is similar to the actions in the front pike and bent-knee variant positions. The center of gravity is somewhat closer to the center of buoyancy than in the pike, but it is somewhat farther from the center of buoyancy than in the bent-knee variant. Therefore, the position of the forearms and palms is somewhere between that of the other two positions (Figure 4-20).

Figure 4-20

Teaching Progression

The same wall drill that was used for the front pike can be used for the crane, with the exception that one leg is lifted to the vertical. Support can be given at the hips or on the ankle of the vertical leg (Figures 4-21, 4-22).

Figure 4-21

Common Errors

1. The swimmer pushes the vertical leg back too far, causing the body to tip over or to be thrown into an arch.
2. The swimmer stretches the vertical leg too far toward the ceiling, causing the body to tip toward the horizontal leg.

Figure 4-22

INVERTED VERTICAL

Sculling Action

To support a vertical position, the elbows are flexed approximately 90 degrees and are close to the waist. The forearms and palms move first away from and then toward the midline of the body in a figure-eight action (Figure 4-23).

Teaching Progression

The swimmer must be able to assume a good vertical. She can practice the position against the wall while a partner supports her ankles. To check the amount of stretch, the coach can grasp the toes of the swimmer and attempt to turn her. If she turns easily, she is stretched sufficiently. Once the swimmer can assume a tight, stretched vertical at the side of the pool, check to see if she can maintain the position away from the wall. When she accomplishes a good vertical position she can begin work on support sculling. Hint: To prevent any arching, tell the swimmer to keep her head in line and contract her abdominals.

Common Errors

1. The swimmer looks at the bottom or does not fully extend, causing an arch.

Figure 4-23

Remind the swimmer to keep her head in line and contract her abdominals.

2. The swimmer is piked at the hips. Tell the swimmer to contract her buttocks and press her hips forward.

3. The swimmer stretches one leg higher than another, causing the body to fall to one side. If she falls to the right, tell her to press her right leg to the left and vice versa.

Chapter 5

AN INTRODUCTION TO MOVEMENT PROGRESSIONS FOR FIGURES

Movement progressions are combinations of body positions, component parts of figures, and related movements which are listed and analyzed in sequential order. The progressions start from simple movements inherent within the basic skills and move to the more complex. A swimmer who is initially taught by the use of movement progressions will become more aware of her capabilities for further skill development. She will then be able to choose those movements that she can perform successfully.

A movement progression approach to teaching synchronized swimming allows for individual differences very early in the development of skills. It also helps the swimmer become more aware of her own movement capabilities.

As the swimmer moves through the progressions, she learns the basic concepts relative to each movement. This knowledge will enable her to avoid mistakes that might be costly in executing the more complex figures. For example, if the pike down-front is learned, then figures utilizing that movement will be more easily acquired and will have fewer mistakes.

There are only a few established movement transitions which can be used to move a body from one position to another. Once the swimmer learns these transitions, she can use them to build her repertoire of figures. For example, when a swimmer learns the front press bent-knee movement, she uses that movement to execute the swordfish, the swordasub, and the swordalina. When a swimmer learns the side ballet-leg, surface, movement, she uses that movement to execute the ballet-leg roll, single, the Eiffel tower, and the Eiffel walk.

Movement Progression Outline
1. *Ballet-Leg*
   a. Ballet-leg, single
   b. Ballet-leg, single, submarine
   c. Side ballet-leg, submerged
   d. T position, submerged
   e. Ballet-leg roll, single
   f. Side ballet-leg, surface
   g. T position, surface
   h. Crane
   i. Ballet-leg, tip back
   j. Ballet-leg, tip up
   k. Ballet-legs, double
   l. Ballet-legs, double, submarine
   m. Ballet-legs roll, double
2. *Tuck*
   a. Tub
   b. Tuck on back, surface
   c. Back tuck somersault
   d. Inverted tuck
   e. Tuck on front, surface
   f. Front tuck somersault
3. *Pike*
   a. Pike drop-back
   b. Back pike somersault
   c. Pike down-front
   d. Front pike
   e. Front pike somersault

35

4. *Arched*
   a. Shark circle
   b. Dolphin
   c. Dolphin feetfirst
   d. Dolphin feetfirst to vertical
   e. Dolphin feetfirst to bent-knee variant
   f. Dolphin feetfirst to crane
   g. Front press bent knee
   h. Front press straight leg
   i. Arch to vertical
5. *Rotational Movements*
   a. Surface twist—water wheel
   b. Catalina rotation
   c. Catalina reverse rotation
   d. Swordalina rotation
   e. Pirouette rotation
   f. Gaviata rotation
   g. Bent-knee half twist
   h. Bent-knee full twist
   i. Vertical half twist
   j. Vertical full twist
   k. Crane twist
   l. Bent-knee 180-degree spin
   m. Bent-knee 360-degree spin
   n. Vertical 180-degree spin
   o. Vertical 360-degree spin
   p. Albatross 180-degree spin
   q. Albatross 360-degree spin
   r. Closed spin
   s. Open spin
6. *Lifting and Unrolling Movements*
   a. Inverted tuck to vertical
   b. Heron unroll
   c. Barracuda unroll
   d. Flamingo bent-knee unroll
   e. Flamingo unroll
   f. Aurora lift
7. *Transitional Movements*
   a. Ballet-legs, double, submarine to ballet-leg, single, submarine
   b. Walk-out, front
   c. Walk-out, back
   d. Front pike to crane
   e. Front pike to vertical
   f. Front pike to bent-knee variant
   g. Vertical to pike
   h. Albatross roll
   i. Knight press back to bent knee

j. Crane to vertical
k. Crane to split
l. Castle press back
m. Pirouette change
n. Side leg lift

ANALYSIS AND APPLICATION TO TEACHING

Movements and sculling transitions within a figure such as the Eiffel tower are nothing more than combinations taught earlier within the progressions.

Eiffel Tower Analysis

1. Body positions
   a. Layout, back
   b. Ballet-leg, single
   c. Front pike
   d. Crane
   e. Inverted vertical
2. Movement progression
   a. Ballet-leg, single
   b. Side ballet-leg, surface
   c. Side ballet-leg, surface, to pike down-front
   d. Front pike
   e. Front pike to crane
   f. Crane
   g. Crane to vertical
3. Sculling (combining basic body positions and movement progressions)
   a. Layout, back—hands at the side, stationary scull, basic figure-eight (Figure 5-1).

Figure 5-1

   b. Ballet-leg, single—the weight of the leg out of the water will increase the need for sculling force; therefore, the speed of the scull and the angle of the palm are increased (Figure 5-2).
   c. Ballet-leg, single, to side ballet-leg, surface—sculling hand on the ballet-leg side sculls behind the hip

Figure 5-2

Figure 5-3

Figure 5-4

until the pike down-front occurs (Figure 5-3). Non-ballet-leg hand makes a wider figure-eight scull to support the side ballet-leg, surface, position.

d. Pike down-front—the non-ballet-leg hand sculls out as the pike down-front occurs, then turns over to catch and support, under the knees on the front pike. The hand on the ballet-leg side sculls under the hips as long as possible, then rotates to the front pike position as the ballet-leg meets the non-ballet-leg.

e. Front pike—sculling occurs near the knees in preparation for the crane position (Figure 5-4).

f. Front pike to crane—a feathering action using small sweeping sculls is taken out to the side as the leg is lifted. Support sculling then continues near the horizontal leg (Figure 5-5).

g. Crane to vertical—small C-sweep sculls to the side as the leg is lifted. The last scull should be completed as both legs meet. Sustained maximum height is desirable; therefore, the hands are near the chest region for the best support (Figure 5-6).

Figure 5-5

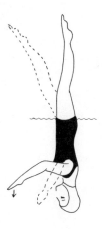

Figure 5-6

Somersub Analysis

1. Body positions
   a. Layout, front
   b. Front pike
   c. Ballet-legs, double
   d. Ballet-leg, single
2. Movement progression
   a. Pike down-front
   b. Front pike
   c. Front pike somersault to ballet-legs, double, submarine
   d. Ballet-legs, double, submarine to ballet-leg, single, submarine
   e. Ballet-leg, single
3. Sculling (combining basic body positions and movement progressions)
   a. Layout, front—sculling (Figure 5-7).
   b. Pike down-front (Figure 5-8).
   c. Front pike somersault to ballet-legs, double, submarine—hands press up toward the head as the hips are rotated. Sculling transfers to hips after the press (Figures 5-9, 5-10, 5-11).

d. Ballet-legs, double, submarine to ballet-leg, single, submarine—hands are transferred from the hips (palms down) to the shoulders (palms up)(Figure 5-12).
e. Ballet-leg, single, submarine, to ballet-leg, single—hands are transferred from the stabilizing position to above the knee on the extended leg. A scull or pressing action will raise the body to the ballet-leg, single, position (Figure 5-13).
f. The hands will automatically end in a ballet-leg, single, sculling position as the body reaches the surface (Figure 5-14).

The analysis of the Eiffel tower and the somersub points out the advantage of using movement progressions which incorporate the basic body positions, basic sculling, and sculling transitions. It should be apparent to the reader that this type of analysis can be done by the swimmer once the progressions are learned.

Figure 5-7

Figure 5-8

Figure 5-9

Figure 5-10

Figure 5-11

Figure 5-12

Figure 5-13

Figure 5-14

Chapter 6

BALLET-LEG MOVEMENT PROGRESSIONS

1. BALLET-LEG, SINGLE

The swimmer assumes a layout, back, position. In this position, the center of gravity is approximately at the pelvic region; therefore, the sculling action must be near the hips and directing force toward the bottom of the pool. If there is insufficient sculling force, the body will rotate, causing the feet to sink.

To maintain a high elevation in the water, the swimmer extends the body completely, with the head in line, the shoulders pressed back, and the buttocks contracted and pressed upward. The swimmer must take air into the lungs, and not the stomach. This extended body position must be maintained throughout the ballet-leg, single, movement (Figure 6-1).

As the swimmer begins to draw the ballet-leg to the bent-knee variant, back position, her knee lifts out of the water. It becomes much heavier and is difficult to support. To create more force, she increases the speed of the scull and the angle of her palms. Throughout the draw, the toe of the ballet-leg is near the medial surface of the extended leg. A conscious attempt is made to press the heel of the ballet-leg upward (Figure 6-2).

Once the bent-knee variant, back, position is assumed, the swimmer stops drawing the knee toward the chest and concentrates on slowly pressing the heel of the bent knee upward to extend the knee (Figure 6-3).

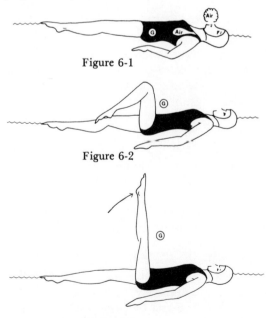

Figure 6-1

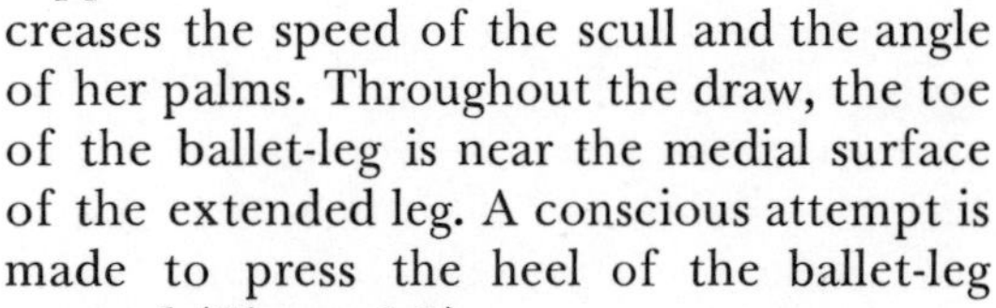

Figure 6-2

Figure 6-3

41

The most difficult phase of the ballet-leg, single, is the knee flexion when returning to the bent-knee variant, back, position. During this phase there is a tendency for the hips to drop. At this point the swimmer must press her hips upward as she increases the speed of the scull and the angle of the palms. The bent knee slowly extends until a layout, back, is assumed.

2. BALLET-LEG, SINGLE, SUBMARINE

The swimmer assumes a ballet-leg, single, position (Figure 6-4). The swimmer initiates the submarine movement by decreasing the speed of the scull and the angle of the palms on both the outward and inward sweeps. The weight of the ballet-leg submerges the swimmer and just enough sculling speed and palm angle are used to control the speed of the drop (Figure 6-5).

As the swimmer submerges, she must consciously press her shoulders and horizontal leg down to prevent piking at the hips. Once the water level is at the ankle of the ballet-leg the swimmer increases the speed of the scull to maintain this submerged position. If the swimmer wishes to return to the ballet-leg, single, position, she simply increases the speed of her scull.

3. SIDE BALLET-LEG, SUBMERGED (RIGHT BALLET-LEG)

The swimmer assumes a ballet-leg, single, submerged, position, with the water level at the ankle. Because all but the foot of the swimmer is submerged, very little sculling force is needed to support this position (Figure 6-6).

Assuming the right leg is the ballet-leg, the roll to the side ballet-leg, submerged, is made by sculling with the right hand at the right hip and the left hand extended in line with the shoulder. The palms are facing in the direction opposite to the desired roll (Figure 6-7).

Throughout this roll, the body must be extended. Care must be taken not to let the shoulders dive toward the bottom of the pool. This dive can be prevented by pressing the shoulders back and sculling with the

Figure 6-4

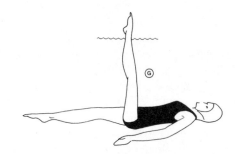

Figure 6-5

Figure 6-6

Figure 6-7

left hand. Once the ballet-leg is parallel to the surface of the water, the palms of the hands are shifted to face the bottom of the pool.

4. T POSITION, SUBMERGED (RIGHT BALLET-LEG)

The swimmer assumes a side ballet-leg, submerged, position. To prevent rotation of the ballet-leg toward the bottom of the pool, most of the sculling action comes from the left hand and forearm.

The roll to the T position, submerged, is made by changing the position of the palms so that they face the direction opposite to the desired roll. The left hand is extended in line with the left shoulder and is used to prevent the shoulders from dropping. The right hand is at the right hip to assist with the roll (Figure 6-8).

The weight of the ballet-leg rolls the body to the T position, submerged. When this position is attained, both hands move somewhere between the shoulders and hips, with the palms facing the bottom and sculling to prevent the shoulders from dropping downward (Figure 6-9).

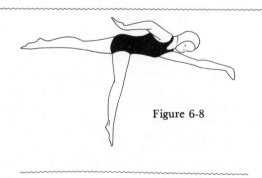

Figure 6-8

Figure 6-9

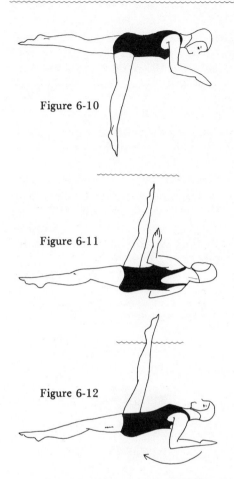

Figure 6-10

Figure 6-11

Figure 6-12

5. BALLET-LEG ROLL (RIGHT BALLET-LEG)

The swimmer assumes a T position, submerged. Because the entire body is submerged, very little sculling force is needed to maintain the position. The hands are somewhere between the shoulders and hips, with the palms toward the bottom of the pool (Figure 6-10).

To initiate the roll to the ballet-leg, single, submarine, position, the left hand moves to the left hip and the right hand moves to the right shoulder. The sculling action is performed with the palms facing the direction opposite to the desired roll. Once the ballet-leg, single, submarine, position is attained, both hands move to the hips with the palms toward the bottom of the pool (Figures 6-11, 6-12).

6. SIDE BALLET-LEG, SURFACE (LEFT BALLET-LEG)

The swimmer assumes a ballet-leg, single, position. In this position, the speed of the scull is rapid, and the palm angle is great in order to support the increased weight of the ballet-leg.

The roll to the side ballet-leg, surface, is made by changing the position of the palms so that they face the direction opposite to the desired roll. The right hand sculls somewhere between the right hip and waist and prevents the ballet-leg from traveling too quickly. The left hand sculls the ballet-leg around to the surface of the water. Throughout the roll, the body must remain fully extended (Figure 6-13).

Figure 6-15

8. CRANE

The swimmer assumes a crane position. The sculling action is described in Chapter 4, page 33 (Figure 6-16).

Figure 6-13

7. T POSITION, SURFACE

The swimmer assumes a layout, front, position. The sculling action is near the hips, with the palms facing the bottom of the pool and the fingertips toward the feet (Figure 6-14).

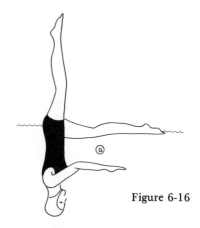

Figure 6-16

9. BALLET-LEG TIP BACK

The swimmer assumes a ballet-leg, single, position (Figure 6-17). To initiate the tip back, the swimmer extends the ballet-leg upward and presses the shoulders and head back and down toward the bottom of the

Figure 6-14

As the T position is assumed, one leg moves toward the bottom of the pool until it is perpendicular to the body. To prevent the feet from sinking, the swimmer keeps her hands at her hips and slightly increases the sculling speed (Figure 6-15).

Figure 6-17

pool (Figure 6-18). The hands scull at the hips until the horizontal leg is vertical and the ballet-leg is on the surface of the water. The fingertips then sweep in toward the body and make a catch to support the crane position (Figures 6-19, 6-20).

10. BALLET-LEG TIP UP

The swimmer assumes a T position, submerged. The arms are extended so that the fingertips are pointing down toward the bottom of the pool (Figure 6-21). To initiate the tip up, the swimmer leads with the little fingers and makes a large circular sweep up toward the surface of the water and then back toward the hips. As the arms are pressing up and back, the shoulders are moving slightly forward and down, and the horizontal leg is moving to a vertical position. The hands and forearms continue the press until the backs of the hands are by the knees and the crane position is assumed (Figures 6-22, 6-23, 6-24, 6-25, 6-26).

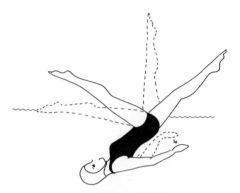

Figure 6-18

Figure 6-19

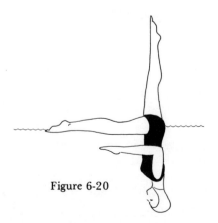

Figure 6-20

Figure 6-21

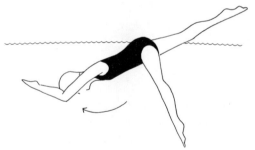

Figure 6-22

Figure 6-23

Figure 6-24

Figure 6-25

Figure 6-26

11. BALLET-LEGS, DOUBLE

The swimmer assumes a layout, back, position (Figure 6-27). As the legs are drawn toward the chest, the knees are brought out of the water, and increased sculling force is needed (Figure 6-28). When the thighs of both legs are perpendicular to the surface of the water, the swimmer stops drawing them toward the chest and concentrates on slowly pressing the heels of both feet upward until the knees are extended. The speed of the scull and the angle of the palms continue to increase as both of the legs lift out of the water (Figure 6-29).

Figure 6-27

Figure 6-28

Figure 6-29

The most difficult phase of the ballet-legs, double, is the knee flexion when returning the feet to the surface of the water. During this phase there is a tendency for the hips to drop. As this point the swimmer must press her hips upward. The bent knees slowly extend until a layout, back, is assumed.

12. BALLET-LEGS, DOUBLE, SUBMARINE

The swimmer assumes a ballet-legs, double, position (Figure 6-30). She initiates the submarine movement by decreasing the speed of the scull and the angle of the palms on both the outward and inward sweeps. The weight of the legs submerges the swimmer, and just enough sculling speed and palm angle are used to control the speed of the drop.

As the swimmer submerges, she must consciously press her shoulders back. Once the water level is at the ankles of the ballet-legs, the swimmer increases the speed of the scull and the angle of the palms to maintain this submerged position (Figure 6-31). If the swimmer wishes to return to the ballet-legs, double, position, she simply increases the speed of her scull and the angle of the palms on the sculling action.

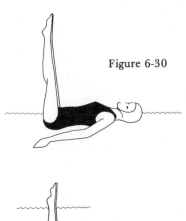

Figure 6-30

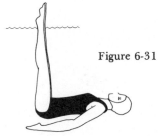

Figure 6-31

13. BALLET-LEGS ROLL, DOUBLE (TO LEFT)

The swimmer assumes a ballet-legs, double, submarine, position (Figure 6-32). The roll to the left is made by sculling with the right hand by the right hip and the left

hand at the left shoulder. The palms are facing in the direction opposite to the desired roll (Figure 6-33).

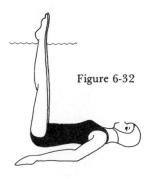

Figure 6-32

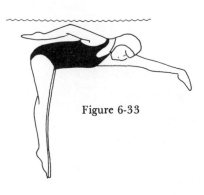

Figure 6-33

Throughout this roll, the body must be extended. Care must be taken not to let the shoulders dive toward the bottom of the pool. This dive can be prevented by pressing the shoulders back and sculling with the left hand.

Once the ballet-legs are perpendicular to the surface of the water, both hands move to a position somewhere near the shoulders (Figure 6-34). To initiate the roll to the ballet-leg, double, submarine, the left hand moves to the left hip and the right hand moves to the right shoulder. The sculling action is performed with the palms facing the direction opposite to the desired roll (Figure 6-35). Once the ballet-legs, double, submarine, position is attained, both hands move to the hips with the palms toward the bottom of the pool (Figures 6-36, 6-37).

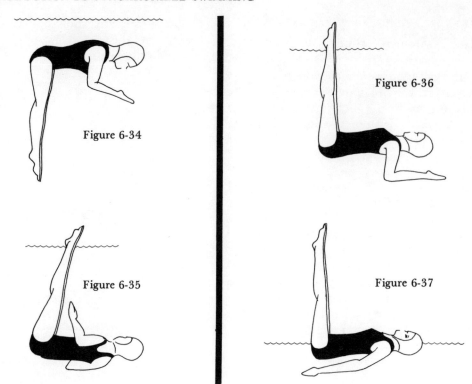

Figure 6-34

Figure 6-36

Figure 6-35

Figure 6-37

Chapter 7

TUCK MOVEMENT PROGRESSIONS

Tub
Tuck on Back, Surface
Back Tuck Somersault
Inverted Tuck
Tuck on Front, Surface
Front Tuck Somersault

1. TUB

The swimmer assumes a layout, back, position (Figure 7-1). As she begins to draw her knees toward her chest, the hips are allowed to drop below the surface of the water. Throughout this draw, the heels must be pressed up so that the legs from the knees to the toes are perpendicular to the surface of the water. The forearms and hands continue to scull at the hips (Figure 7-2, 7-3).

The swimmer then changes the angle of her palms so that one wrist is flexed and one is hyperextended. She uses a headfirst sculling action with one hand and a feet-first sculling action with the other hand until one revolution is made (Figures 7-4, 7-5).

Upon completion of the revolution, the swimmer returns both the hands to the standard sculling action at the hips. The body is then slowly extended to a layout, back, position (Figure 7-6, 7-7).

2. TUCK ON BACK, SURFACE

The swimmer assumes a layout, back, position (Figure 7-8). She draws her knees toward her chest as in the tub position

Figure 7-1

Figure 7-2

Figure 7-3

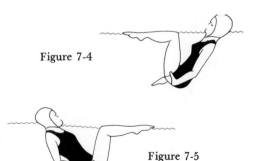

Figure 7-4

Figure 7-5

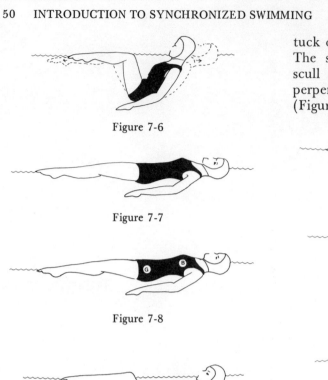

Figure 7-6

Figure 7-7

Figure 7-8

Figure 7-9

Figure 7-10

tuck on back, surface (Figures 7-12, 7-13). The shoulders press back and the hands scull at the hips until the lower legs are perpendicular to the surface of the water (Figures 7-14, 7-15). The momentum and

Figure 7-11

Figure 7-12

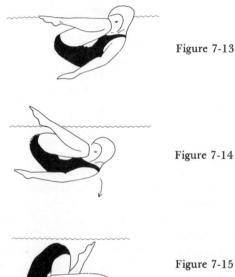

Figure 7-13

Figure 7-14

Figure 7-15

(Figure 7-9). The chin is tucked, and the knees continue the draw until they contact the forehead. In this tight tuck position, the center of gravity is very close to the center of buoyancy; therefore, the hands move out to the side and scull somewhere between the waist and hips to prevent rotation (Figure 7-10).

3. BACK TUCK SOMERSAULT

The swimmer assumes a layout, back, position (Figure 7-11). She then executes a

buoyancy of the body carry it around, and the hands merely scull at the hips to prevent too rapid a rotation (Figure 7-16). When the momentum of the body slows down, the hands scull at the hips until a tuck on back, surface, is assumed (Figure 7-17). The swimmer then extends to a

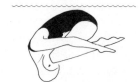

Figure 7-16

Figure 7-17

Figure 7-18

Figure 7-19

Figure 7-20

Figure 7-21

Figure 7-22

Figure 7-23

Figure 7-24

Figure 7-25

layout, back, position, with her hands sculling at the hips (Figure 7-18).

4. INVERTED TUCK

The swimmer assumes a layout, back, position (Figure 7-19). She then executes a partial back tuck somersault until her lower legs are perpendicular to the surface of the water (Figures 7-20, 7-21). The hands make a small circular sweep (catch or C-sweep) with the fingertips leading in toward the hips (Figure 7-22). The technique used to sustain the inverted tuck is support sculling (Figure 7-23).

5. TUCK ON FRONT, SURFACE

The swimmer assumes a layout, front, position, with her hands sculling at her hips (Figure 7-24). She continues to scull at her hips as she tucks her chin and draws her knees toward her chest until her forehead contacts her knees. In this tight tuck position, the hands move out to the side and scull somewhere between the waist and hips to prevent rotation (Figure 7-25).

6. FRONT TUCK SOMERSAULT

The swimmer assumes a layout, front, position with her hands sculling at her hips (Figure 7-26). As she executes a tuck on front, surface, she uses an arm action as described in the pike down-front to create forward momentum (Figures 7-27, 7-28). This momentum and the buoyancy of the body carry it around, and the hands merely scull at the hips to prevent too rapid a rotation (Figure 7-29). When the momentum of the body stops, the hands scull at the hips until a tuck on front, surface, is assumed (Figure 7-30). The swimmer then extends to a layout, front, position with her hands sculling at the hips.

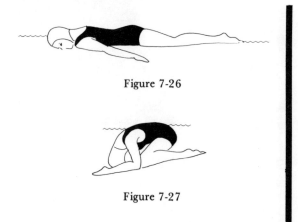

Figure 7-26

Figure 7-27

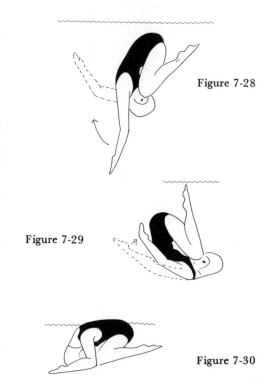

Figure 7-28

Figure 7-29

Figure 7-30

Chapter 8

PIKE MOVEMENT PROGRESSIONS

Pike Drop-back
Back Pike Somersault
Pike Down-front
Front Pike
Front Pike Somersault

1. PIKE DROP-BACK

The swimmer assumes a layout, back, position (Figure 8-1). To start the pike drop-back, the hands flip over so that the palms are toward the surface of the water. The thumbs lead as the arms slice back toward the shoulders and angle slightly down toward the bottom of the pool (Figure 8-2). At the same time, the legs are lifted toward the head. The weight of the lifted legs and the loss of sculling force will submerge the body. The abdominals are contracted, and legs and ankles are extended so that a tight pike position can be assumed and maintained (Figure 8-3).

2. BACK PIKE SOMERSAULT

The swimmer assumes a layout, back, position (Figure 8-4). She then executes a pike drop-back (Figures 8-5, 8-6), and as she submerges, she presses her forearms and hands in a circular movement up toward the surface and back toward her feet (Figure 8-7). This movement causes the body to rotate backward. When the momentum of the body slows down, the hands scull at the hips until the toes and head break the surface of the water

Figure 8-1

Figure 8-2

Figure 8-3

Figure 8-4

Figure 8-5

Figure 8-6

53

Figure 8-7

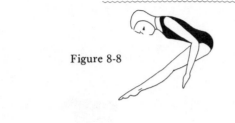

Figure 8-8

Figure 8-9

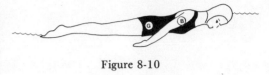

Figure 8-10

Figure 8-11

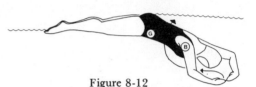

Figure 8-12

Figure 8-13

Figure 8-14

(Figures 8-8, 8-9). The swimmer then extends to a layout, back, position.

3. PIKE DOWN-FRONT

The swimmer assumes a layout, front, position (Figure 8-10). To start the pike down-front, the swimmer slices her arms and hands down toward the bottom of the pool (Figure 8-11). The wrists flex and the palms sweep up toward the surface of the water. As the chest is pressed forward and the abdominals contract, the elbows flex and the hands sweep in a circular motion (Figure 8-12).

As the body nears a 90-degree pike, the hands scull toward the surface with the arms reaching back behind the shoulders. The fingertips slice through the water, catch, and support scull (Figures 8-13, 8-14).

4. FRONT PIKE

The swimmer assumes a layout, front, position (Figure 8-15). She then executes a pike down-front until the body nears a 90-degree inverted pike (Figures 8-16, 8-17, 8-18). The technique used to sustain the front pike is support sculling (Figure 8-19).

5. FRONT PIKE SOMERSAULT

The swimmer assumes a layout, front, position (Figure 8-20). She then executes a pike down-front until the body assumes a 90-degree front pike (Figures 8-21, 8-22, 8-23, 8-24). Maintaining the pike, she uses

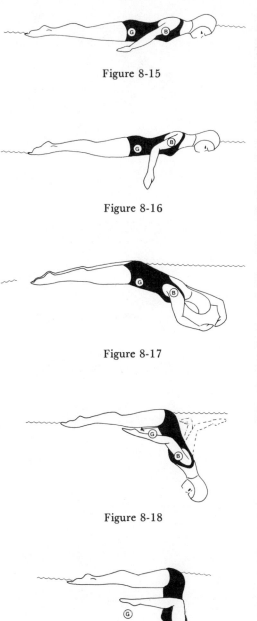

Figure 8-15

Figure 8-16

Figure 8-17

Figure 8-18

Figure 8-19

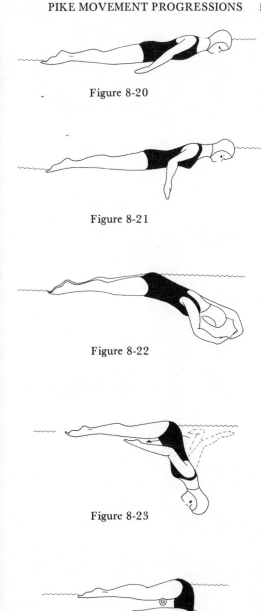

Figure 8-20

Figure 8-21

Figure 8-22

Figure 8-23

Figure 8-24

an additional press and turnover of the hands to move from the front pike to a ballet-legs, double, submarine, position (Figures 8-25, 8-26, 8-27).

The hands flip over so that the palms are toward the surface. Another circular sweep is used to press the body around so that the back is at the surface of the water and the legs are perpendicular (Figures 8-28, 8-29). The hands scull at the hips as the heels are pressed up. The swimmer then assumes a layout, front, position.

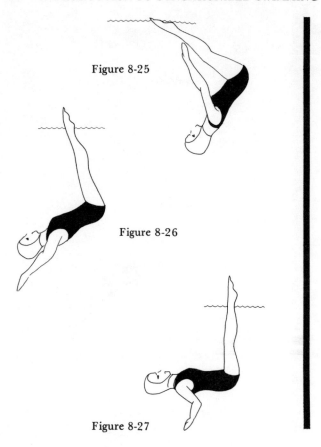

Figure 8-25

Figure 8-26

Figure 8-27

Figure 8-28

Figure 8-29

Chapter 9

ARCHED MOVEMENT PROGRESSIONS

Figure 9-1

1. SHARK CIRCLE (ON RIGHT SIDE)

The swimmer assumes a layout, back, position. She rolls onto her right side by lifting her left hip and shoulder. The top arm extends fully overhead in line with the body, palm toward the bottom and the forearm and hand parallel to the surface of the water. To maintain a high elevation in the water, the body must be completely extended with the head in line, the right ear in the water, the shoulders pressed back, the buttocks contracted and pressed forward, and the ankle of the bottom leg pressed upward against the top leg. As the swimmer begins the circle, the lower back arches slightly and the heels press back and up. Throughout the shark circle, the body position must be maintained (Figures 9-1, 9-2). The sculling action for the side scull—layout, side—is used for propulsion. (For a description see Chapter 4, page 30.)

The circumference of the circle will vary with the size of the swimmer. A taller swimmer will make a larger circle. If the swimmer wishes to decrease the size of the

Figure 9-2

circle, all she has to do is increase the arch in her back and press her heels back a little farther (Figure 9-3).

2. DOLPHIN

The swimmer assumes a layout, back, position. The hands then flip over so that the palms are away from the bottom of the pool, and the thumbs lead as the arms slice through the water to an extended position

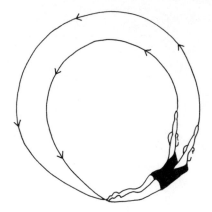

Figure 9-3

water. As the body begins to descend head-first, the pitch of the hands becomes less, and the arms begin to move to the front of the body and toward the waist (Figures 9-6, 9-7).

Figure 9-6

Figure 9-7

overhead (Figure 9-4). Because the sculling force diminishes at this point, the swimmer must forcefully press her heels up to prevent their sinking (Figure 9-5). The body must be completely extended with the head in line, the shoulders pressed back, and the buttocks contracted and pressed forward. To assist with the correct body position, the swimmer must take air into the lungs and not the stomach.

Figure 9-4

Figure 9-5

The arms and hands are the body parts which create the force to propel the body headfirst in the dolphin. The sculling action for headfirst scull—layout, back (hands overhead) is used here. (For a description, see Chapter 4, page 29.) The shoulders press back, and the back arches. The swimmer continues to press her heels upward so that they remain on the surface of the

When the head passes the halfway point of the circle, the hands are sculling at the hips with the thumbs by the hips, the palms toward the feet, and the fingertips toward the bottom of the pool. As the swimmer begins to move toward the surface of the water, she uses the buoyancy of her body to carry her upward. The sculling force is directed upward to prevent the body from rising too quickly and is accomplished by keeping the elbows in close to the waist and the forearms and hands angled toward the surface and away from the front of the body. This scull is continued until the head breaks the surface of the water.

As the head breaks the surface, the hands flip over so that the palms are down toward the bottom and angled slightly toward the feet. A headfirst scull (see Chapter 4, page 29) is then used as the arch is decreased in the lower back. The swimmer then assumes a layout, back, and continues moving headfirst (Figure 9-8).

Figure 9-8

The circumference of the circle varies with the height of the swimmer and the amount of arch in her back. Throughout the circle, it is important that the head, hips, and feet touch the circumference of the circle.

3. DOLPHIN FEETFIRST

The swimmer assumes a layout, back, position. The feetfirst movement is initiated by using the feetfirst scull—layout, back (hands near the hips). (For a description, see Chapter 4, page 29.) As the swimmer moves feetfirst, she begins to press her heels down. She continues the scull as she arches her lower and then upper back. Just before her head submerges, she makes a catch by leading with her thumb toward her hips and then rotates her forearm so that her fingers brush past her hips. Her hands are then in front of her body, with the palms toward the surface of the water.

The swimmer begins a feathering action that can be defined as a series of rapid outward and inward sculling movements: the fingertips point away from the face and the forearms and the hands move from hip to above head level. The feathering action continues as the feet, hips, and head follow

the circumference of a circle and the toes break the surface of the water. The forearms and hands then shift to an overhead scull. The swimmer should use the buoyancy of her body to carry her upward and use the scull only to keep her moving feetfirst. When the feet break the surface, the heels press up. The arch is broken by extending first the lower back and finally the upper back. The swimmer then assumes a layout, back, position and continues moving feetfirst (Figure 9-9).

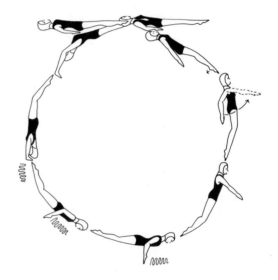

Figure 9-9

The circumference of the circle varies with the height of the swimmer and the amount of arch. The taller swimmer will make a larger circumference than a shorter swimmer.

4. DOLPHIN FEETFIRST TO VERTICAL

The swimmer assumes a layout, back, position. From this position she executes a dolphin feetfirst until her feet pass the three-quarter point of the circumference of the circle. At this point she takes the arch out of her body by pressing her heels slightly forward, extending her lower back and finally her upper back. The swimmer should use the buoyancy of her body to carry her upward and employ the scull only to control her vertical body position at the final desired height (Figure 9-10). The sculling action is that described for the inverted vertical position in the sculling for support section of Chapter 4, page 34 (Figure 9-11).

It is extremely important that a good vertical position be maintained. An arched position can be prevented by keeping the head in line and contracting the abdominals. A pike position can be prevented by contracting the buttocks.

Figure 9-10   Figure 9-12   Figure 9-14

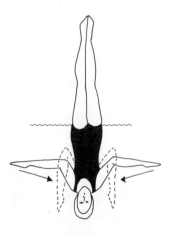

Figure 9-11

5. DOLPHIN FEETFIRST TO BENT-KNEE VARIANT

The swimmer assumes a layout, back, position. From this position she executes a dolphin feetfirst to a vertical position. As the toes break the surface of the water, the hands move to a support scull position and the swimmer assumes a bent-knee variant position (Figures 9-12, 9-13).

Figure 9-13

6. DOLPHIN FEETFIRST TO CRANE

The swimmer assumes a layout, back, position. From this position she executes a dolphin feetfirst to a vertical position. As the toes break the surface of the water, the hands move to a support scull position and the swimmer assumes a crane position (Figures 9-14, 9-15).

Figure 9-15

7. FRONT PRESS BENT KNEE

The swimmer assumes a bent-knee variant, front, position. In the front press bent-knee movement, the foot of the extended leg will lift out of the water in an arc until the back of the leg reaches the surface of the water. Because the body part is out of the water, a great amount of sculling force must be created to keep the body high in the water.

Figure 9-16

Before initiation of the movement, the swimmer presses her shoulders down toward the bottom of the pool. She extends her arms toward her feet with the palms toward the pool bottom (Figure 9-16). In one smooth continuous motion, she arches her lower and upper back, presses the heel of her extended leg toward her head, and uses a feathering action of her arms and forearms almost directly under the midline of her body. One feathering action from the hips to overhead should be enough to carry the vertical leg over the water and onto the surface. If another feathering action is needed, the elbows quickly flex and move toward the midline of the body, and the hands recover back to the hips. The feathering action is then repeated (Figures 9-17, 9-18).

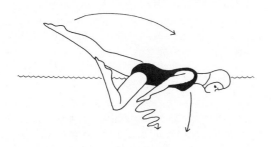

Figure 9-17

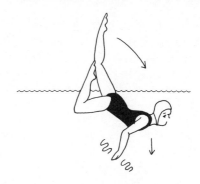

Figure 9-18

Figure 9-19

Once the heel of the vertical leg reaches the surface of the water, the forearms and hands shift to an overhead scull (Figure 9-19). The swimmer should use the buoyancy of her body to carry her upward and use the scull only to keep her moving feetfirst.

When the heel of the vertical leg reaches the surface of the water, the heel presses up. The bent knee slowly extends as the arch is broken by extending first the lower back and finally the upper back. The swimmer then assumes a layout, back, position.

8. FRONT PRESS STRAIGHT LEG

The swimmer assumes a layout, front, position. In the front press straight leg, one leg will lift out of the water in an arc until the heel reaches the surface of the water. Then the second leg lifts out of the water and meets the first leg. Because the body parts are moving out of the water, a great amount of sculling force must be created to keep the body high in the water.

Before beginning the first press, the swimmer presses her shoulders down toward the bottom of the pool. She extends her arms toward her feet with the palms toward the bottom of the pool (Figure 9-20). In one smooth continuous motion, she arches her lower and upper back, presses the heel of one leg toward her head, and uses the feathering action described for the front press bent knee (Figure 9-21).

Once the heel of the vertical leg reaches the surface of the water, the forearms and hands shift to an overhead scull. The swimmer is now supporting a split position in the vertical plane.

The hands and forearms slice through the water and scull directly under the second leg. The hands are located somewhere between the foot and knee of the second leg with the palms toward the bottom of the pool (Figure 9-22).

Figure 9-20

Figure 9-21

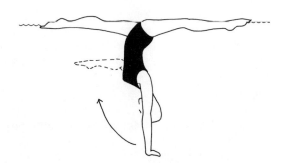

Figure 9-22

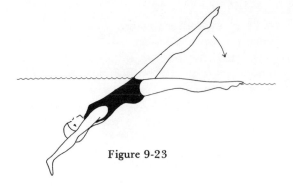

Figure 9-23

Figure 9-24

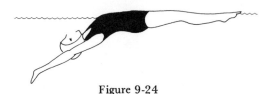

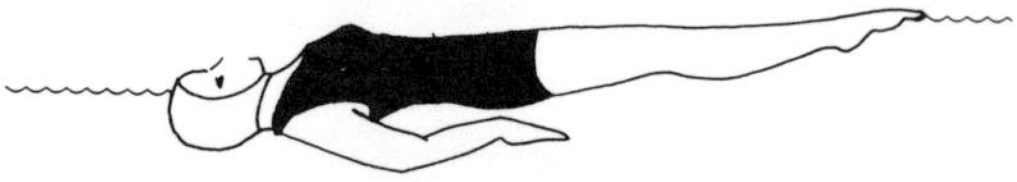

Figure 9-25

In one smooth continuous motion, the swimmer presses the heel of the second leg toward the first leg and uses the feathering action to lift the second leg over to meet the first leg. The forearms and hands then shift to an overhead scull (Figure 9-23). The swimmer should use the buoyancy of her body to carry her upward and employ the scull only to keep her moving feetfirst (Figure 9-24).

When both legs meet, the heels press up and the arch is broken by extending first the lower and finally the upper back. The swimmer then assumes a layout, back, position (Figure 9-25).

9. ARCH TO VERTICAL

The swimmer assumes a layout, back, position (Figure 9-26). She then executes a dolphin until her head reaches the one-quarter point of the circumference of the circle (Figures 9-27, 9-28). At this time she sculls back behind her shoulders and as close to the backs of the knees as possible. As she presses both heels upward, and contracts her abdominals and buttocks, she sculls with her palms toward the bottom of the pool. When the swimmer reaches the vertical, she uses a support sculling action, as described in Chapter 4, page 34 (Figure 9-29).

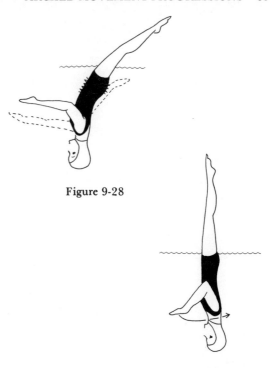

Figure 9-28

Figure 9-26

Figure 9-27

Figure 9-29

Chapter 10

ROTATIONAL MOVEMENT PROGRESSIONS

1. SURFACE TWIST—WATER WHEEL

The swimmer assumes a layout, back, position. As the twist is started, the hands stop the sculling action and just the legs and feet propel the body around in a circle. Because the sculling force diminishes at this point, the swimmer must forcefully press her heels up to prevent them from sinking. The body must be completely extended with the head in line, the shoulders pressed back, and the buttocks contracted. The position of the arms and hands is optional, but a favorite position is with one hand at the hip and the other at the back of the head.

The twist is accomplished by using a pedaling action with the feet and legs. The ankles are flexed as they recover forward and extend as they press the water in the direction opposite to the desired movement. When the circle is completed, the swimmer assumes a layout, back, position (Figure 10-1).

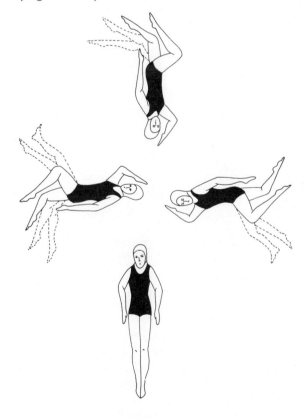

Figure 10-1

2. CATALINA ROTATION (RIGHT BALLET-LEG)

The swimmer assumes a right ballet-leg, single, position (Figure 10-2). During the rotation, force must be applied toward the bottom of the pool and under the vertical leg.

To begin the rotation, the swimmer tucks her chin, rounds her back, and presses her shoulders down and toward the hip of the horizontal leg (Figure 10-3). The left hand sculls at the left hip, and the right hand reaches away from the right hip and out to the right side. The right palm angles slightly away from the body to help press the shoulders around under the hips.

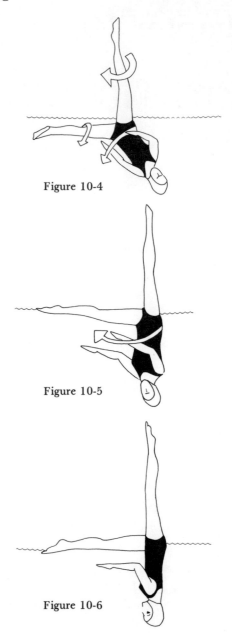

Figure 10-4

Figure 10-5

Figure 10-6

Figure 10-2

Figure 10-3

Throughout this action, the right leg rotates medially and the left leg rotates laterally simultaneously (Figure 10-4). When the shoulders are almost directly under the hips, both hands make a catch and the right hand sculls from the position behind the body to a position at the hip

(Figure 10-5). A supported crane position is then assumed (Figure 10-6).

3. CATALINA REVERSE ROTATION (RIGHT BALLET-LEG)

The swimmer assumes a crane position with the right leg vertical (Figure 10-7). The sculling action must be well under the horizontal leg to stabilize the crane position and to prevent the body from rotating from this position. Throughout the rotation, force must be applied toward the bottom of the pool and under the vertical leg.

To begin the rotation the swimmer tucks her chin, rounds her back, and presses her shoulders up toward the hip of the vertical leg (Figure 10-8). To help press the shoulders around and up toward the surface of the water, the right hand support sculls at the right hip while the left hand support sculls slightly out from the left hip.

Throughout this action, the right leg rotates laterally and the left leg rotates medially simultaneously (Figure 10-9). As the shoulders move toward the surface, the hands rotate to a sculling position at the hips (Figure 10-10). The back continues to round forward and press up toward the vertical leg (Figure 10-11). The swimmer assumes a ballet-leg, single, position (Figure 10-12).

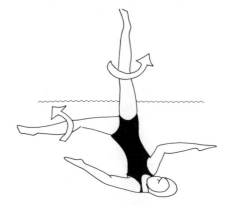

Figure 10-9

Figure 10-10

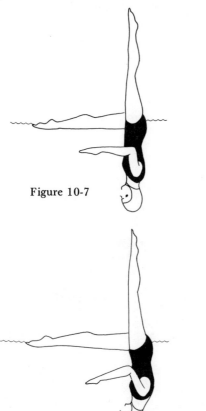

Figure 10-7

Figure 10-11

Figure 10-8

Figure 10-12

4. SWORDALINA ROTATION (RIGHT LEG VERTICAL)

The swimmer assumes a bent-knee variant, front, position (Figure 10-13). She then executes a front press bent knee until her head is directly under the foot of the extended leg (Figure 10-14).

To begin the rotation, the swimmer tucks her chin, rounds her back, and presses her shoulders up toward the hip of the vertical leg. The right hand support sculls out from the right hip to assist with the rotation while the left hand support sculls at the left hip. At the same time the vertical leg rotates medially and flexes at the hip so that it remains perpendicular to the surface of the water (Figure 10-15).

As the shoulders move toward the surface, the hands rotate to a sculling position at the hips. The back continues to round forward and the shoulders press up toward the vertical leg (Figure 10-16). The swimmer assumes a flamingo position (Figure 10-17).

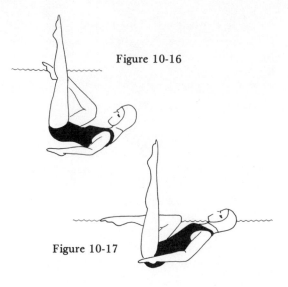

Figure 10-16

Figure 10-17

Figure 10-13

Figure 10-14   Figure 10-15

5. PIROUETTE ROTATION (LEFT LEG)

The swimmer assumes a left ballet-leg, single, position (Figure 10-18). To begin the rotation the swimmer rotates her trunk so that the left shoulder moves to the right, the backs of her shoulders press toward the surface of the water, and her back arches. The right hand sculls at the hip, and the left hand reaches away from the left hip and out to the left side. The left palm angles slightly away from the body to assist with the shoulder rotation.

Figure 10-18

Throughout this action the left leg rotates medially and the right leg rotates laterally simultaneously (Figure 10-19). When the shoulders are near the surface of the water, both hands make a catch, and the left hand sculls from the position behind the body to a position at the hip. A

Figure 10-19

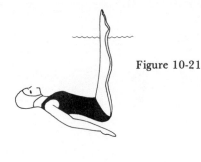

Figure 10-21

Figure 10-20

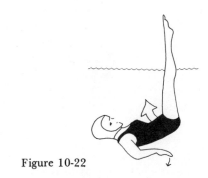

Figure 10-22

supported crane position with the back arched is then assumed (Figure 10-20).

6. GAVIATA ROTATION (RIGHT LEG FORWARD)

The swimmer assumes a ballet-legs, double, submerged, position (Figure 10-21). The speed of the scull and the angle of the palms are increased so that the body rises. The chin is tucked, the back is rounded, the shoulders are pressed back, the abdominals are contracted, and the buttocks are contracted and pressed forward as the forearms and hands press out and down toward the bottom of the pool (Figure 10-22).

To begin the rotation, the swimmer tucks her chin and presses her shoulders toward the left hip (Figure 10-23). The left hand sculls at the left hip and the right hand reaches away from the right hip and out to the right side. The right palm angles slightly away from the body to help press the shoulder under the hips (Figure 10-24).

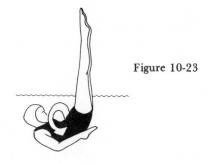

Figure 10-23

Figure 10-24

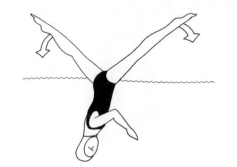

Figure 10-25

Figure 10-26

position. She should assume a vertical position with her feet toward the bottom of the pool in the deep water. The elbows should be in close to the waist and flexed approximately 90 degrees. The hands and forearms move toward and away from each other at the side of the body in a plane parallel to the surface of the water. To assist the twist, the swimmer angles the palms of the hands in a direction opposite to the desired movement (Figures 10-27, 10-28, 10-29, 10-30).

After the swimmer gets the feel of the twist, she can attempt the twist in various inverted positions. If she experiences difficulty in the position, she may then return to this drill. (Example: If she is having difficulty with the crane twist, let her try the crane twist with her feet toward the bottom of the pool.)

Just prior to the completion of the rotation, the back arches, the right leg is flexed, and the left leg is hyperextended (Figure 10-25). The swimmer then assumes a supported split position (Figure 10-26).

TWISTS AND SPINS

Once the swimmer can support the basic synchronized swimming positions with a fair amount of control, she can add a twist or spin action. A twist is a slow controlled rotation of the body while maintaining a constant water level somewhere between the ankles and knees. The twist must be completed before the heels drop below the surface of the water. A spin is a rapid rotation about the body, which is started at the height of a lift or unroll, which continues as the body descends, and which is completed before the heels drop below the surface of the water.

Because the twist is a slower action, it is usually easier to learn than the spin. The swimmer should get the feel of the movement before attempting it in an inverted

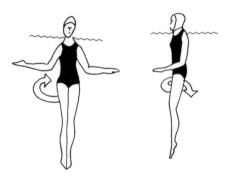

Figure 10-27   Figure 10-28

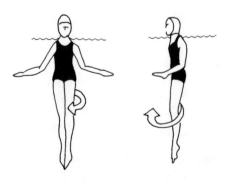

Figure 10-29   Figure 10-30

7. BENT-KNEE HALF TWIST

The swimmer assumes a bent-knee variant position and support sculls. To assist the turn, the palms of the hands angle in the direction opposite to the desired movement. The sculling action continues until the body rotates 180 degrees (Figures 10-31, 10-32, 10-33).

Care must be taken to maintain the bent-knee variant position in the vertical plane. Pressing the heel of the vertical leg back will cause an arched body position because of the weight of the bent knee. Relaxing or arching in the position will cause the vertical leg to loop around on the surface of the water.

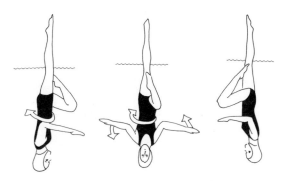

Figure 10-31   Figure 10-32   Figure 10-33

8. BENT-KNEE FULL TWIST

The swimmer assumes a bent-knee variant position. The same sculling action is used as in the bent-knee half twist. This sculling action continues until the body rotates 360 degrees.

9. VERTICAL HALF TWIST

The swimmer assumes an inverted vertical position. It is easier for beginners to attain a vertical position without dropping by extending slowly. It is easier for them to stop completely before attempting a twist. To prevent excessive arching, the swimmer contracts the abdominals and pulls the head in line with the body. To prevent excessive piking, she contracts the buttocks (Figure 10-34).

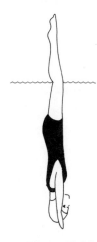

Figure 10-34

The upper arms are extended from the shoulders and parallel to the surface of the water. The elbows are flexed 90 degrees. The forearms and hands are perpendicular to the surface of the water and in line with the ears. Movement of the hands and fore-arms is in a vertical plane toward and away from the ears. To assist the turn, the palms of the hands angle slightly in the direction opposite to the desired movement. The sculling action continues until the body rotates 180 degrees (Figures 10-35, 10-36, 10-37).

Figure 10-35   Figure 10-36   Figure 10-37

The swimmer must not attempt to turn the body by rotating just the hips. Sculling more forcefully with one hand than the other will cause an uneven or jerky turn. If the palms angle toward the bottom of the pool, the body will bob up and down. Relaxing or arching the body causes the legs to loop around on the surface of the water.

10. VERTICAL FULL TWIST

The swimmer assumes an inverted vertical position. The same sculling action is used as in the vertical half twist. This sculling action continues until the body rotates 360 degrees.

11. CRANE TWIST

The swimmer assumes a crane position (Figure 10-38). Be sure the horizontal leg is perpendicular to the body. A common mistake is letting the foot of the horizontal leg come up to the surface of the water.

Figure 10-39

Figure 10-40

Figure 10-41

Figure 10-38

The action of the forearms and hands is similar to that in the bent-knee twist. Because the center of gravity is out slightly farther from the midline of the body than in the bent knee, the hands reach out farther toward the feet. The twist is executed by angling the palms of the hands in the direction slightly opposite to the desired rotation and by pressing the inside of the horizontal leg against the vertical leg (Figures 10-39, 10-40).

Spin Action

The action of the arms and hands is similar for most spins. To get the feel of the spin, the swimmer should begin in the deep water in a vertical position with her feet toward the bottom of the pool. The elbows should be in close to the waist and flexed approximately 90 degrees. When attempting to spin to the right (right shoulder pressing back), the swimmer should press the right arm and forearm across the front of the body toward the left shoulder. The left elbow flexes, and the thumb slices through the water toward the left ear. This action should spin the body and must be practiced before the swimmer attempts inverted spins from a lift or unroll (Figure 10-41).

12. BENT-KNEE 180-DEGREE SPIN

The swimmer assumes a bent-knee variant position. If a spin to the right is desired, the right arm and forearm press across the front of the body toward the left shoulder. The left elbow flexes and the thumb slices through the water toward the left ear. This action should rotate the body 180 degrees (Figure 10-42). The water level must remain constant throughout the 180-degree rotation. Upon completion of the 180-degree rotation, a catch is made and support sculling is used (Figure 10-43).

Figure 10-44   Figure 10-45

action is the same as in the bent-knee 180-degree spin. The water level must remain constant throughout the 180-degree rotation (Figure 10-46). Upon completion of the 180-degree rotation, a catch is made and support sculling is used (Figure 10-47).

Figure 10-42   Figure 10-43

13. BENT-KNEE 360-DEGREE SPIN

The swimmer assumes a bent-knee variant position. The same press is used as in the bent-knee 180-degree spin. Both hands use a sculling action to continue the rotation (Figures 10-44, 10-45).

14. VERTICAL 180-DEGREE SPIN

The swimmer assumes an inverted vertical position. This is usually the most difficult spin to execute because a good vertical position must be maintained. The arm

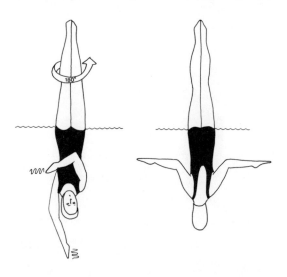

Figure 10-46   Figure 10-47

15. VERTICAL 360-DEGREE SPIN

The swimmer assumes an inverted vertical position. The arm action is the same as in the bent-knee 360-degree spin (Figures 10-48, 10-49).

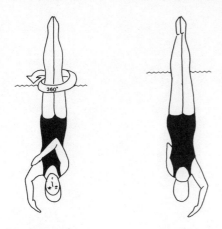

Figure 10-48   Figure 10-49

17. ALBATROSS 360-DEGREE SPIN

The swimmer assumes a bent-knee variant position (Figure 10-53). The arm action is the same as in the bent-knee 360-degree spin. During the spin, the knee and hip of the bent leg slowly extend to the vertical (Figures 10-54, 10-55, 10-56).

Figure 10-53   Figure 10-54

16. ALBATROSS 180-DEGREE SPIN

The swimmer assumes a bent-knee variant position (Figure 10-50). The arm action is the same as in the bent-knee 180-degree spin. During the spin, the knee and hip of the bent leg slowly extend to the vertical (Figures 10-51, 10-52).

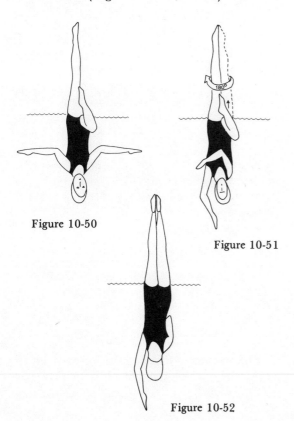

Figure 10-50

Figure 10-51

Figure 10-52

Figure 10-55   Figure 10-56

18. CLOSED SPIN

The swimmer assumes a split position using the sculling action described in Chapter 4, page 32 (Figure 10-57). To initiate the spin, both legs move up and in until a vertical position is assumed. The closed-spin action occurs because of a continuous and steady leg action and hip rotation (Figures 10-58, 10-59).

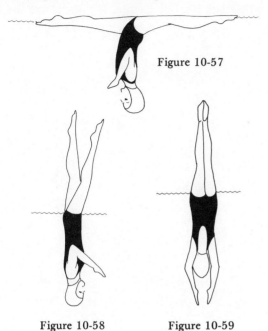

Figure 10-57

Figure 10-58   Figure 10-59

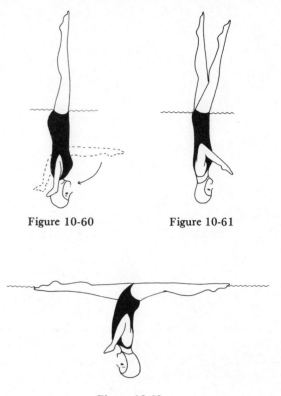

Figure 10-60   Figure 10-61

Figure 10-62

19. OPEN SPIN

The swimmer assumes an inverted vertical position, using the sculling action described in Chapter 4, page 34 (Figure 10-60). To initiate the spin, both legs move down and out until a split position is assumed (Figures 10-61, 10-62). The open-spin action occurs because of a continuous and steady leg action and hip rotation. The greater the amount of stretch in the split, the higher the elevation.

amount of stretch in the split, the higher the elevation.

The sculling action moves with the open spin. The scull moves from the sides of the body to an overhead position. Constant pressure toward the bottom of the pool should be maintained. The arm that is applying force in the direction opposite to the spin will cross the body. The other arm continues to scull toward the bottom of the pool.

Chapter 11

LIFTING AND UNROLLING MOVEMENT PROGRESSIONS

Inverted Tuck to Vertical
Heron Unroll
Barracuda Unroll
Flamingo Bent-Knee Unroll
Flamingo Unroll
Aurora Lift

1. INVERTED TUCK TO VERTICAL

The swimmer assumes an inverted tuck position (Figure 11-1). A feathering action is used as she extends her hips and knees to a vertical position. This feathering action can be defined as a series of rapid outward and inward sculling movements with the fingertips pointing away from the face, and the forearms and hands moving from a position at the hips to a position out from the shoulders (Figures 11-2, 11-3).

2. HERON UNROLL

The swimmer assumes a submerged flamingo position (Figure 11-4). The chin is tucked, the back is rounded, the shoulders are pressed back, the abdominals are contracted, and the buttocks are contracted and pressed forward as the forearms and hands press out and down toward the bottom of the pool (Figure 11-5). When the hands reach hip level, the body should be extended in a bent-knee variant position. The hands make a small circular sweep (C-sweep), with the fingertips leading in toward the hips; support sculling for the bent-knee variant is used (see Chapter 4, page 32). The shoulders and head are the last to come into line (Figure 11-6).

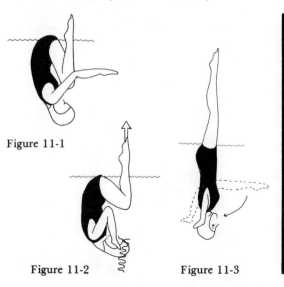

Figure 11-1

Figure 11-2

Figure 11-3

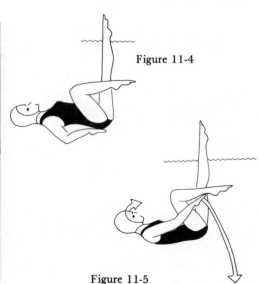

Figure 11-4

Figure 11-5

Figure 11-6

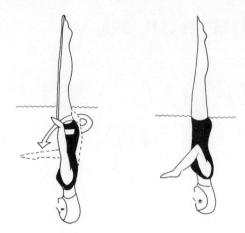

Figure 11-9   Figure 11-10

3. BARRACUDA UNROLL

The swimmer assumes a ballet-legs, double, position (Figure 11-7). The speed of the scull is increased so that the body rises toward the surface of the water. The hands then reach toward the knees. The chin is tucked, the back is rounded, the shoulders are pressed back, the abdominals are contracted, and the buttocks are contracted and pressed forward as the forearms and hands press out and down toward the bottom of the pool (Figure 11-8).

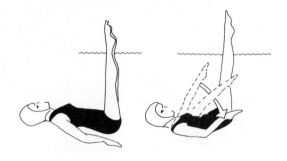

Figure 11-7   Figure 11-8

When the hands reach hip level, the body should be completely extended. The hands make a small circular sweep (C-sweep), with the fingertips leading in toward the hips to a support sculling position (Figure 11-9). The shoulders and head are the last to come into line (Figure 11-10).

4. FLAMINGO BENT-KNEE UNROLL

The swimmer assumes a flamingo position (Figure 11-11). The chin is tucked, the back is rounded, the shoulders are pressed back, the abdominals are contracted, and the buttocks are contracted and pressed forward as the hands and forearms continue to scull at the hips (Figure 11-12). As the head and shoulders press back, the body assumes a bent-knee variant position. When the head and shoulders are in line with the hips, the hands make a small circular sweep (C-sweep), with the fingertips leading in toward the hips. The swimmer then supports the bent-knee variant position (Figure 11-13).

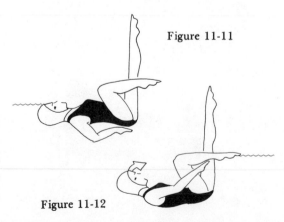

Figure 11-11

Figure 11-12

Figure 11-13

5. FLAMINGO UNROLL

The swimmer assumes a ballet-legs, double, position (Figure 11-14). The chin is tucked, the back is rounded, the shoulders are pressed back, the abdominals are contracted, and the buttocks are contracted and pressed forward as the hands and forearms continue to scull at the hips (Figure 11-15). When the head and shoulders are in line with the hips, the hands make a small circular sweep (C-sweep), with the fingertips leading in toward the hips. The swimmer then supports the inverted vertical position (Figure 11-16).

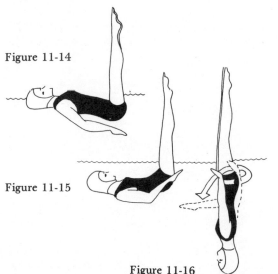

Figure 11-14

Figure 11-15

Figure 11-16

6. AURORA LIFT

The swimmer assumes a ballet-legs, double, submerged, position (Figure 11-17). The speed of the scull is increased so that the body rises. The back is rounded, the chin is tucked, the abdominals are contracted, and the buttocks are contracted and pressed forward to begin the lift (Figure 11-18). The lower back then arches, and one leg is hyperextended so that the knee, ankle, and foot are in line and parallel to the surface of the water. As the leg hyperextends, the scull is well under this leg with the palms toward the bottom.

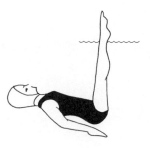

Figure 11-17

Figure 11-18

To raise the body higher, the swimmer presses the forearms and hands down and then makes a catch by rotating the fingertips toward the body so that the scull is in front of the shoulders (Figure 11-19). A supported knight position is then assumed (Figure 11-20).

Figure 11-19

Figure 11-20

Chapter 12

TRANSITIONAL MOVEMENT PROGRESSIONS

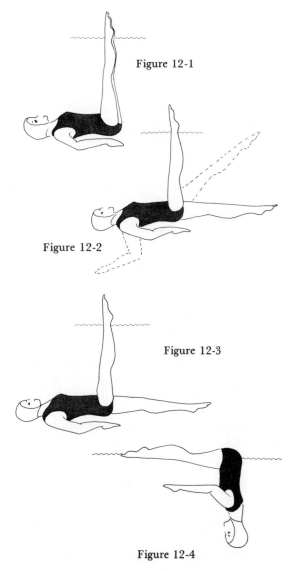

Figure 12-1

Figure 12-2

Figure 12-3

Figure 12-4

1. BALLET-LEGS, DOUBLE, SUBMARINE, TO BALLET-LEG, SINGLE, SUBMARINE

The swimmer assumes a ballet-legs, double, submarine (Figure 12-1). The hands are transferred from sculling at the hips, palms down, to the shoulder, palms up. At the same time one leg is pressed down to a horizontal position (Figure 12-2). The swimmer then assumes a ballet-leg, single, submarine (Figure 12-3).

2. WALK-OUT, FRONT

The swimmer assumes a front pike position (Figure 12-4). In the walk-out, front, one leg will lift out of the water in an arc until the back of the heel reaches the surface of the water. Then the second leg lifts out of the water and meets the first leg. Because the body parts are moving out

81

of the water, a great amount of sculling force must be created to keep the body high in the water.

To start the lift, the swimmer presses one heel toward her head and arches the lower back. As she presses the heel up out of the water, she uses a feathering action to create enough force to lift the leg.

Once the heel of the vertical leg reaches the surface of the water, the forearms and hands shift to an overhead scull with the palms toward the bottom of the pool. The swimmer is now supporting a split position (Figure 12-5).

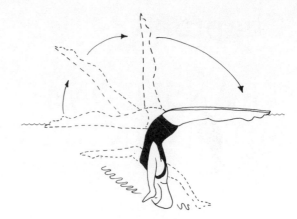

Figure 12-6

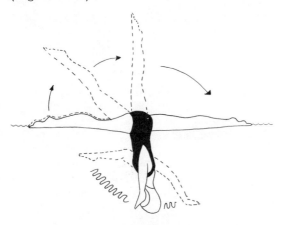

Figure 12-5

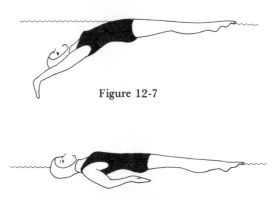

Figure 12-7

Figure 12-8

The hands and forearms slice through the water and scull directly under the second leg. The hands are located somewhere between the foot and knee of the second leg with the palms toward the bottom of the pool.

In one smooth continuous motion, the swimmer presses the heel of the second leg toward her head and uses the feathering action to lift the leg over to meet the first leg (Figure 12-6). The forearms and hands then shift to an overhead scull (Figure 12-7). The swimmer should use the buoyancy of her body to carry her upward and use the scull only to keep her moving feetfirst.

When both legs meet, the heels press up and the arch is broken by extending first the lower and finally the upper back. The swimmer then assumes a layout, back, position (Figure 12-8).

3. WALK-OUT, BACK

The body assumes a layout, back, position (Figure 12-9). A dolphin movement is started until the head is directly under the hips (Figure 12-10). At this time, the swimmer sculls back behind her shoulders and as close to the backs of the knees as possible. As she presses one heel upward, she sculls with her palms toward the bottom of the pool and moves her hands to a position overhead. The swimmer is now supporting a split position (Figure 12-11).

The hands and forearms slice through the water and scull directly under the knee of the second leg. As the second leg is pressed over the surface of the water to meet the first leg, the same sculling action

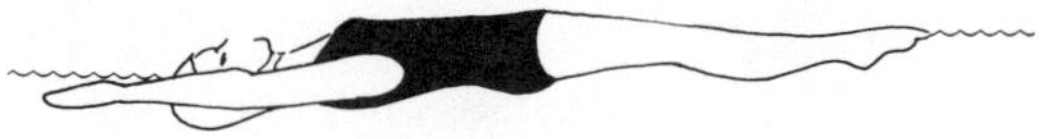

Figure 12-9

Figure 12-10

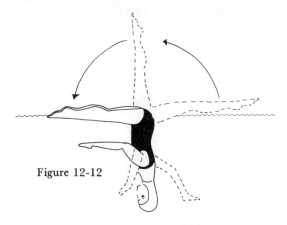

Figure 12-12

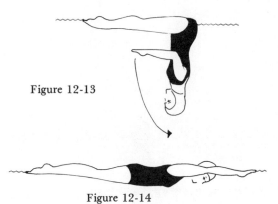

Figure 12-13

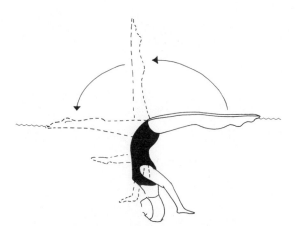

Figure 12-11

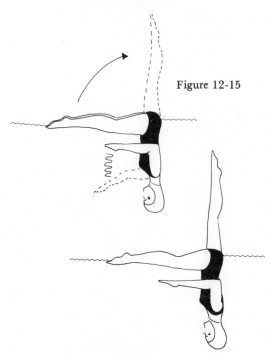

Figure 12-14

Figure 12-15

is used (Figure 12-12). The legs meet and a front pike is assumed (Figure 12-13). The forearms and hands then shift to an overhead scull. The swimmer should use the buoyancy of her body to carry her upward and use the scull only to keep her body moving feetfirst.

The pike is broken by contracting the abdominals and buttocks. The swimmer then assumes a layout, front, position (Figure 12-14).

4. FRONT PIKE TO CRANE

The swimmer assumes a front pike position. She uses a feathering action as she presses one leg up to the vertical (Figure 12-15). The swimmer then support sculls in the crane position (Figure 12-16).

Figure 12-16

5. FRONT PIKE TO VERTICAL

The swimmer assumes a front pike position. She uses a feathering action as she presses both legs up to the vertical. The swimmer then support sculls the vertical position (Figure 12-17).

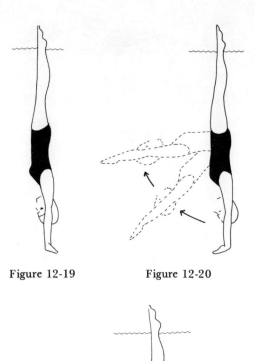

Figure 12-19   Figure 12-20

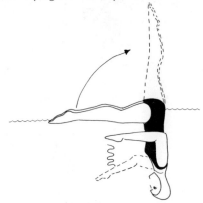

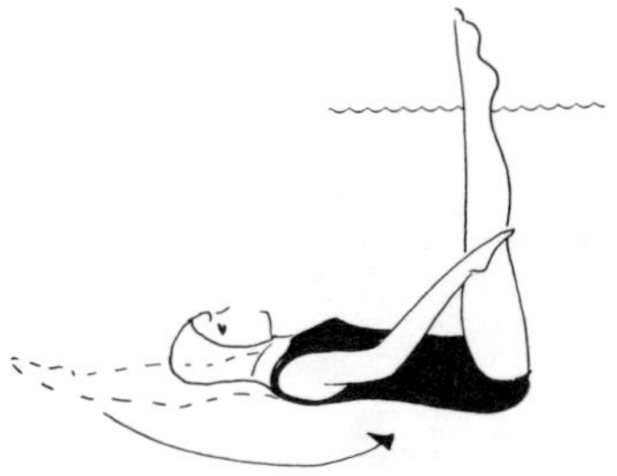

Figure 12-17

6. FRONT PIKE TO BENT-KNEE VARIANT

The swimmer assumes a front pike position. She uses a feathering action as she presses one leg up to the vertical and the other leg to a bent-knee position. The swimmer then supports the bent-knee variant (Figure 12-18).

Figure 12-21

head (Figure 12-19). It is important that the swimmer learn to contract the abdominal muscles to initiate the pike action. The body pikes up slowly as the shoulders move toward the surface of the water.

The sculling action begins by rotating the arms and hands toward the hips. Short, small sculls out to the side are done to stabilize the body as it is piking up (Figure 12-20). As the body reaches the ballet-legs, double, submerged, position, the scull is taken out to the side and near the knees. A regular ballet-legs, double, scull is assumed (Figure 12-21).

Figure 12-18

7. VERTICAL TO PIKE

The swimmer assumes an inverted vertical position. Both hands scull above the

8. ALBATROSS ROLL

The swimmer assumes a layout, back, position (Figure 12-22). The dolphin is started and, upon submergence of the head, the right shoulder presses down toward the bottom of the pool. The elbow of the right

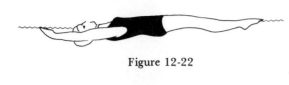

Figure 12-22

Figure 12-23

Figure 12-24

Figure 12-25

Figure 12-26

Figure 12-27

arm is dropped in next to the side of the body (Figure 12-23). The left shoulder continues to move as the abdominal muscles contract, and the body assumes a front pike position (Figure 12-24).

9. KNIGHT PRESS BACK TO BENT-KNEE

The swimmer assumes a ballet-leg, single, position (Figure 12-25). The chin is tucked and the shoulders rounded as the hips are pressed up. The shoulders press back hard to the knight position as the hip of the ballet-leg is pressed away from the movement. The horizontal leg remains on the surface of the water (Figure 12-26). As the head comes under the hip, the vertical leg is brought to the bent-knee position, and the horizontal leg is lifted to the vertical.

The sculling action starts with the hands by the hips in the ballet-leg, single, position. As the body moves back through the knight position, the sculling stays by the hips as long as possible. The catch occurs with the fingertips leading in toward the midline of the body (C-sweep). The swimmer then supports the bent-knee variant position (Figure 12-27).

10. CRANE TO VERTICAL

The swimmer assumes a crane position (Figure 12-28). She uses a feathering action as she presses the horizontal leg up to the vertical. She then supports the inverted vertical position (Figure 12-29).

Figure 12-28

Figure 12-29

Figure 12-30

Figure 12-31

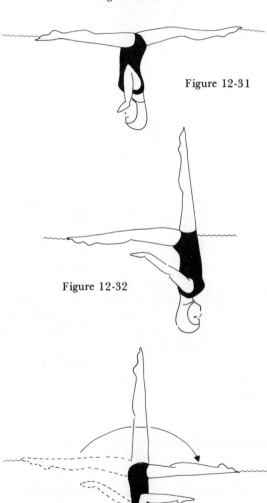

Figure 12-32

Figure 12-33

11. CRANE TO SPLIT

The swimmer assumes a crane position. To start the lift to the split, she presses the heel of the vertical leg away from the horizontal leg and arches the lower back. As she presses the leg over, she uses a feathering action to create enough force to keep the body high in the water (Figure 12-30). The swimmer then assumes a split position (Figure 12-31).

12. CASTLE PRESS BACK

The swimmer executes a knight press back to the knight position (Figure 12-32). After the knight position is assumed, the horizontal leg is brought through an arc to the crane position. The sculling action during this change is a catch (C-sweep). Strong, continuous support sculls are executed during the leg change. The swimmer then supports the crane position (Figure 12-33).

13. PIROUETTE CHANGE

The swimmer assumes an arched crane position (Figure 12-34). The horizontal leg moves in an arc toward the vertical leg. To start the lift, the swimmer presses the heel of the horizontal leg toward her head. As she presses the heel up and out of the water, she uses a feathering action (Figure 12-35). The fingertips point away from the face, and the forearms and the hands move from the hips to above the head. As the horizontal leg passes the vertical leg, the vertical leg is brought to a bent-knee position (Figures 12-36, 12-37).

Figure 12-37

14. SIDE LEG LIFT

The swimmer assumes a layout, side, position. Movement headfirst is initiated with one arm sculling beneath the hip. The other arm is extended overhead. There is lateral flexion of the body as the head and shoulders move toward the bottom of the pool. The top arm is extended with the palm up toward the surface and small reverse sculls are executed so that force is applied toward the surface of the water (Figure 12-38). Prior to the leg lift, the bottom arm sweeps across the body in front of the chest and applies force toward the feet. When the head is beneath the hips both arms press toward the bottom and the legs are lifted to the vertical. As the legs lift through an arc to the vertical a support scull is used (Figure 12-39).

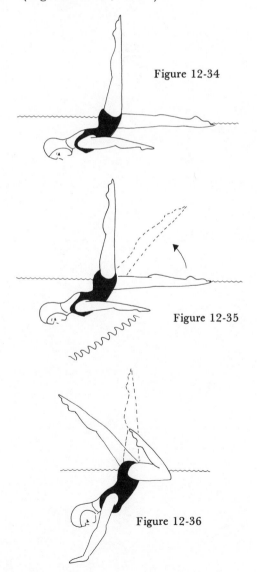

Figure 12-34

Figure 12-35

Figure 12-36

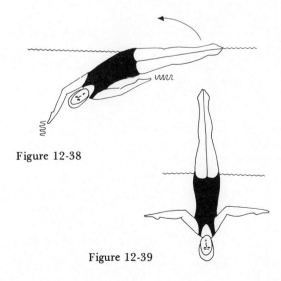

Figure 12-38

Figure 12-39

Chapter 13

DRY-LAND EXERCISES FOR THE SYNCHRONIZED SWIMMER

Dry-land exercise programs, when properly organized, can develop endurance, strength, and flexibility at a much faster rate than just conditioning with a swimming program alone. Another advantage to a dry-land program is that it provides controlled physical conditioning when water time is not available. A good exercise program that is based on circuits or station training can accommodate numerous swimmers while providing for maximum work loads.

Three facets of fitness that are of extreme importance to the synchronized swimmer are strength, flexibility, and endurance. Many of the figures performed in routines or in figure competition demand a great deal of flexibility, especially in using the body positions that are inherent in the figures. Strength is of prime importance due to the power needed for such actions as executing ballet-legs, double; support sculling; and twists and spins. Without good endurance the synchronized swimmer will find it difficult to keep up the pace needed in swimming routines.

For general purposes an effective dry-land exercise program must be designed to provide a balance of conditioning in the fitness areas mentioned above. The coach must be able to recognize which exercises will benefit the swimmer in all three areas. An understanding of what these components of fitness are is also necessary.

Strength: Exerting some force against a resistance.

The only way to build strength is to utilize the overload principle. This principle is primarily concerned with subjecting the muscle or muscle groups to loads that are greater than normal. This should be done with progressively increasing loads. Without proper emphasis on this overload principle in conditioning, the swimmer will not improve. Weight training may have to be used, along with general exercises to achieve success in the area of strength.

Flexibility: Range of motion in a joint.

Flexibility can be easily obtained with consistent exercising. Slow stretching of the muscle to gain flexibility must be controlled, so there is no injury to the swimmer. Stretching by bouncing is detrimental because it is in direct opposition to the stretching action. Static stretching or slowly holding a desired position is best. When doing stretching movements, many quick jerky movements may result in stiffness or sore muscles. It should be noted at this point that weight training is not harmful to flexibility if done properly.

Endurance: Ability to work and continue to work without becoming quickly fatigued.

Developing endurance can be a very complex adventure unless both the coach and the swimmer understand the principles behind endurance training. Too often, synchronized swimmers fail to develop optimum conditioning in this area because of lack of land-training time after the routines are completed. Again, the principle of overload is of prime importance. A swimmer must be pushed to achieve a high level of endurance.

Some of the changes in a well-conditioned synchronized swimmer are:
1. The resting heart rate is lower.
2. The recovery heart rate, after strenuous work is faster.
3. There is a lower heart rate during the training session.

The coach can easily observe the effectiveness of endurance training by taking heart rates on each swimmer.

Interval training is an absolute must in developing endurance. This applies to water conditioning as well as dry-land conditioning. Intervals in exercising depend upon three things: the intensity of the work load, the frequency of the exercise, and the length of the overload. At the start of the season the heart rate should be raised from the resting rate to a rate of 140 beats per minute during the work load. As the swimmer progresses through the season, the heart rate should be raised to 160 to 165 beats per minute.

An example of interval training for dry-land exercises can be described as follows:

Exercise—Running in Place Fast

Work Load		3 minutes
(Set 1)	Repeats	3X3[1] minutes (20 seconds rest between repeats)
	Rest	2 minutes
(Set 2)	Repeats	3X3 minutes (20 seconds rest between repeats)
	Rest	2 minutes

[1] The first number indicates the number of repetitions; the second one indicates the number of repeats or the length of time one must continue each repetition. 3X3 minutes (20 seconds rest between repeats) means:
1. run 3 minutes then rest 20 seconds
2. run 3 minutes then rest 20 seconds
3. run 3 minutes then rest 20 seconds

(Set 3)	Repeats	3X3 minutes (20 seconds rest between repeats)

As the swimmer improves, the rest period between the sets can be shortened. Heart rates should be taken before the swimmers start, after the first rest period, and after the second set.

Any well-designed exercise program should utilize three general methods of exercising. Each method is different and should offer a varied program for the swimmer.

EXERCISE METHODS

Isotonic

This method utilizes muscular contraction with observable movement.
1. Jumping Jacks.   4. Running in Place.
2. Squat-thrusts.   5. Push-ups.
3. Sit-ups.

Isometric

This method utilizes muscular contraction with no observable movement.
1. Sit on floor and contract buttocks. Hold for 5 seconds.
2. Place palms of hands together in front of the chest and press palms against each other. Hold for 5 seconds.
3. Ankle extension. After extending the ankles and arching the foot, hold this position for 5 seconds.
4. Doorway pushes—stand between a doorway, place palms on each side and press. Hold for 5 seconds.
5. Stomach tightening—contract abdominal muscles for 5 seconds, then relax.

Resistance

This method combines general isotonic exercises with the use of weights.
1. Sit-ups—on a slant board with a 5-pound weight behind the head.
2. Push-ups—with a 2½-pound weight belt.
3. Arm flexes—while holding 2½-pound barbells.
4. Leg presses—sitting on a bench and pushing weights forward.

5. Press-ups—sitting position with one 2½-pound barbell in each hand, pressing barbells straight up above head.

A point that should be considered when setting up a program is that isotonic exercises will increase flexibility but isometric exercises will not. Isotonic, isometric, and resistance exercises will develop strength as well as endurance. One advantage of isometric training is that the swimmer can do it without special equipment. All three methods of training should be used in a well-designed dry-land exercise program.

EXERCISES

The following exercises have been designed to provide a wide variety of choices for the coach or the synchronized swimmer. The methods of isotonic and isometric training have been incorporated into these general divisions: the back; the abdominals; the arms, shoulders, and chest; the neck; and the hips and legs. The exercises can be interchanged and used in any sequence; many can be used with or without weights, depending upon the purpose of the exercise—whether it is to build strength or endurance. It is strongly recommended that prior to the start of any program the swimmer should have a complete physical examination by a qualified physician.

A general description of the exercise is provided. A solid line indicates prime movers and a broken line indicates the stabilizer muscle groups being used. All three areas of strength, flexibility, and endurance are included in each group.

Exercises for the Back
1. *Stick Body* (Figure 13-1)
   Head resting on stable support.

Figure 13-1. Stick Body

Arms, trunk, and legs held in straight line.
Hold, relax, and repeat.
2. *Forward Bend* (Figure 13-2)
   Stand erect, feet 10 to 12 inches apart.
   Fingertips touching neck, elbows well back.
   Keep spine and neck straight, flex forward slowly at hips.
   Return slowly, move hips slightly backward.
   Relax and repeat.

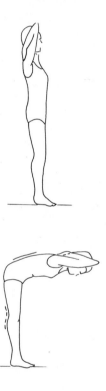

Figure 13-2. Forward Bend

3. *Chin Lifts* (Figure 13-3)
   Lie face down, hands at hips.
   Place hands behind the neck.
   Raise chin until it is about 1 foot off floor. Hold.
   Return to starting position.
   Relax and repeat.

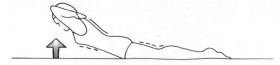

Figure 13-3. Chin Lifts

a.

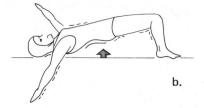

b.

Figures 13-6a, 13-6b. Shoulder Stand

4. *Swan* (Figure 13-4)
   Lie face down, arms extended side-ward from shoulders, palms down.
   Arch back, lifting head, arms, chest, and thighs in extreme extension.
   Return slowly.
   Relax and repeat.

Figure 13-4. Swan

5. *Ankle Clasp* (Figure 13-5)
   Sit with knees spread and flexed, heels close to buttocks.
   Arms reach inside legs, grasp ankles from outside.
   Pull with hands on ankles.
   Draw shoulder blades together.
   Hold, relax, and repeat.

Figure 13-5. Ankle Clasp

6. *Shoulder Stand* (Figures 13-6a, 13-6b)
   Lie on back, arms at side, knees flexed, feet on floor, and heels close to buttocks.
   Pressing on arms, on back of head,

and on feet, lift hips and shoulders off floor to form an arc.
Relax and repeat.

7. *Leg-Arm Stretch* (Figure 13-7)
   Lie face down, legs flat on floor.
   Raise one leg about 15 inches off floor. Return—do with other leg.
   With arms extended overhead, raise one arm off floor, return, repeat with other arm.
   Relax and repeat.

Figure 13-7. Leg-Arm Stretch

8. *Back Arch* (Figure 13-8)
   Lie on back, knees flexed, heels close to buttocks, arms extended sideward, palms down.
   Arching the back, press on the back of the head, the arms, and the hips.
   Contract the back muscles, vigorously drawing the shoulders blades together.
   Relax and repeat.

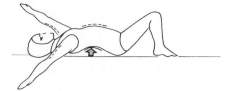

Figure 13-8. Back Arch

9. *Flutter Kick* (Figure 13-9)
   Lie face down, legs flat on floor, hands on back of neck, elbows flexed.
   Raise legs alternately about 1 foot from floor.
   Keep head and chest off floor.
   Do continuously for about thirty counts.
   Relax and repeat.

Figure 13-9. Flutter Kick

10. *Bridge* (Figure 13-10)
    Lie flat on back.
    Flex knees.
    Press up on the back of head.
    Relax and repeat.

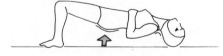

Figure 13-10. Bridge

11. *Back Bend* (Figure 13-11)
    Lie flat on back.
    Press up to a back-bend position.
    Keep hands and feet flat on ground.
    Relax and repeat.

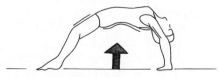

Figure 13-11. Back Bend

12. *Toe Grabs* (Figure 13-12)
    Start in a standing position.
    Slowly go down, grab under toes, and hold.
    Release and uncurl slowly.
    Relax and repeat.

Figure 13-12. Toe Grabs

13. *Back Flings* (Figures 13-13a, 13-13b)
    Sit in tight tuck position, head touching knees.
    Swing arms upward, arch back, and hold.
    Return to tuck position and hold.
    Relax and repeat.

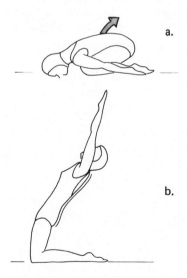

Figures 13-13a, 13-13b. Back Flings

14. *Static Chin-ups* (Figure 13-14)
    Use overhand grip and slowly pull up on a chinning bar.
    Head back, focus up to the ceiling.
    Hold, relax and repeat.

Figure 13-14. Static Chin-ups

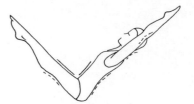

Figure 13-16. V-sit

Abdominal Exercises

1. *Sit-ups with a Twist* (Figure 13-15)
    Lie flat on back, knees flexed, hands behind head, elbows flexed.
    Keeping feet flat, flex spine.
    Touch right elbow to left knee and left elbow to right knee.
    Have partner hold feet.
    Relax and repeat.
    Use a 5-pound weight behind the head for more resistance.

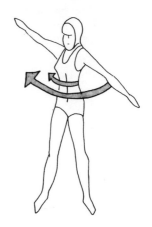

Figure 13-17. Trunk Twist—Arms Extended

Figure 13-15. Sit-ups with a Twist

2. *V-sit* (Figure 13-16)
    Sit on buttocks at 45-degree angle with knees extended, spine slightly flexed, arms extended overhead.
    Hold position for five counts.
    Relax and repeat.
3. *Trunk Twist—Arms Extended* (Figure 13-17)
    Feet flat on floor, legs apart, arms abducted—extended.
    Rotate top part of body to right,

return, then rotate to left, keeping arms abducted and moving only from the waist up.
Relax and repeat.

4. *Toe-touch Sit-ups* (Figures 13-18a, 13-18b)
    Lie on back, legs straight, arms stretched overhead.
    Rise to sitting position.
    Reach forward to touch toes, keeping knees extended.
    Return to straight sitting position.
    Round back and roll down to lying position, raising arms overhead.
    Relax and repeat.
    Do not bounce.
5. *Nutcracker* (Figures 13-19a, 13-19b)
    Lie on back, legs and arms extended.
    Arms are out at shoulder level, palms down.
    Swing leg to left, touching toe lightly to floor as near left hand as possible.

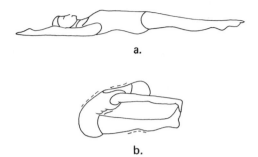

Figures 13-18a, 13-18b. Toe-touch Sit-ups

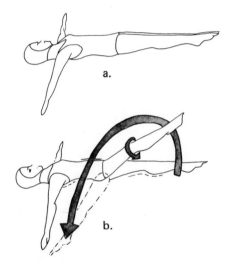

Figures 13-19a, 13-19b. Nutcracker

Return leg to vertical position.
Lower leg, heel touching floor slightly.
Shoulders do not leave the floor throughout the exercise.
Repeat with other leg.
Relax and repeat.

6. *Slow Bent-Knee Doubles* (Figures 13-20a, 13-20b, 13-20c)
Lie on back, knees flexed, feet flat on floor, hands under neck.
Flex both knees to chest.
Straighten legs to bring them to a vertical position.
Keeping knees extended, lower legs to about a 90-degree angle.
Flex knees to put feet on floor.

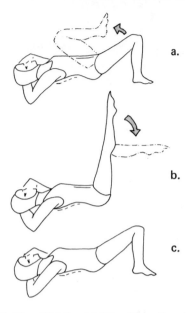

Figures 13-20a, 13-20b, 13-20c. Slow Bent-Knee Doubles.

7. *Abdominal Contraction* (Figure 13-21)
Lie on floor, knees flexed, feet flat.
Contract abdominal wall to flatten it as much as possible.
Hold, relax, and repeat.

Figure 13-21. Abdominal Contraction

8. *Curl* (Figure 13-22)
Lie on back, hands on front of thighs, elbows extended.
Pull chin in, raise head.
Shoulders and back come off the floor.
Return to original position.
Relax and repeat.

Figure 13-22. Curl

9. *Side Scissors Kick* (Figure 13-23)
    Lie on side.
    Swing bottom leg forward, top leg swings backward.
    Keep toes pointed, legs extended.
    Change legs and side positions.
    Point toes while swinging legs.
    Relax and repeat.

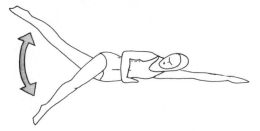

Figure 13-23. Side Scissors Kick

10. *Knee Hug* (Figures 13-24a, 13-24b)
    Lie on back, arms extended overhead.
    Pull trunk up, and knees to chest.
    Clasp ankles with hands.
    Return to starting position.
    Relax and repeat.

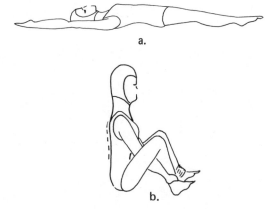

Figures 13-24a, 13-24b. Knee Hug

11. *Crisscross* (Figures 13-25a, 13-26a)
    Sitting position—legs and arms spread.
    Raise legs slightly from floor.
    Crisscross arms and legs.

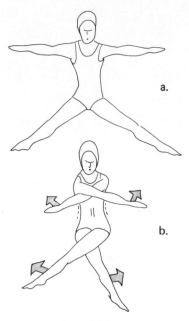

Figures 13-25a, 13-25b. Crisscross

Relax and repeat.
Make sure legs remain off floor.

12. *Trunk Twist* (Figures 13-26a, 13-26b)
    Start in standing erect position, elbows flexed with hands on shoulders.
    Lean forward to a 90-degree angle.
    Twist trunk so that left elbow touches right knee and then right elbow touches left knee.
    Relax and repeat.
    Use abdominal muscles to twist.

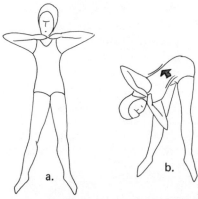

Figures 13-26a, 13-26b. Trunk Twist

13. *Trunk Twist—Standing* (Figures 13-27a, 13-27b)
Start in standing erect position, elbows flexed, hands on shoulders.
Twist right elbow to left side.
Twist left elbow to right side.
Repeat ten times.
Relax and repeat.

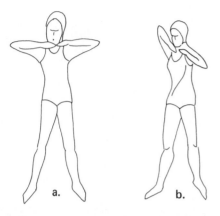

Figures 13-27a, 13-27b. Trunk Twist Standing

14. *Inward-Outward Leg Rotation* (Figure 13-28)
Start lying on back.
Lift right leg, point toe, and circle outward.
Repeat ten times.
Repeat with left leg.
Relax and repeat.

Figure 13-28. Inward-Outward Leg Rotation

15. *Side Splits* (Figure 13-29)
Start lying on side.
Raise top leg and hold.
Repeat ten times.
Change sides and repeat.
Relax and repeat.
Point toes and arch feet.

Figure 13-29. Side Splits

Exercises for Arms, Shoulders, and Chest

1. *Chin-ups* (Figure 13-30)
Stand erect, hands grasping bar with overhand grip.
Pull self up until the chin touches the top of the bar.
of the bar.
Release self slowly.
Relax and repeat.

Figure 13-30. Chin-ups

2. *Push-ups* (Figure 13-31)
Front leaning rest position with the arms extended to support the body weight.
Dip trunk by flexing the elbows until chin touches the floor.
Extend the elbows and push up to the starting position.
Keep the body in a straight line.
Touch only the chin.

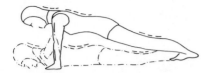

Figure 13-31. Push-ups

3. *Elbow Flings* (Figures 13-32a, 13-32b, 13-32c)
Sit on floor, legs crossed.
Flex elbows to bring fists in front of chest, elbows at shoulder level.
Slowly pinch shoulder blades together.
Keep elbows at shoulder level.
Keep shoulders low and avoid thrusting head forward.
Quickly fling arms so that elbows extend.
Push elbows back as far as possible.
Repeat ten times.
Relax and repeat.

a.

b.

c.

Figures 13-33a, 13-33b, 13-33c. Squat-Thrust with Push-up

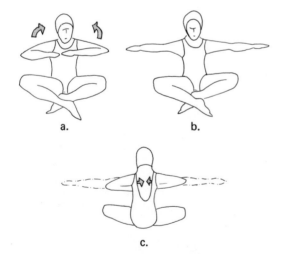

a.   b.

c.

Figures 13-32a, 13-32b, 13-32c. Elbow Flings

4. *Squat-Thrust—with Push-up* (Figures 13-33a, 13-33b, 13-33c)
From standing erect position, drop to a squat, keeping arms on the outside of the knees and hands on the floor.
With a jump, thrust the legs straight out behind body.

Keep body straight, flex elbows, lower body until chest nearly touches the floor.
Push up to front-leaning position.
Return to squat and then stand.
Repeat ten times.
Relax and repeat.

5. *Arm Circler* (Figure 13-34)
Stand erect.
Bring arms in front, swing upward, sideward, and then down.
Relax and repeat.
Arms are swung with a continuous movement.
The circles are made with considerable speed.
Add 5-pound weights for more resistance.

6. *Wing Lift* (Figure 13-35)
Lie face down on floor, arms clasped at back of neck, legs straight, toes touching floor.
Lift arms to press shoulder blades together (hands are behind head),

Figure 13-34. Arm Circler

Figure 13-35. Wing Lift

chest raises as arms pull up.
Hold, relax and repeat.

7. *Ceiling Raiser* (Figures 13-36a, 13-36b)
Stand erect, hands upward (palms up).
Stretch and push upward.

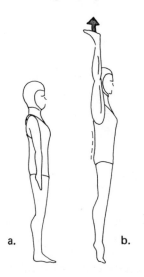

Figures 13-36a, 13-36b. Ceiling Raiser

Go up on toes as push is executed.
Relax and repeat.
Use 5-pound weight for more resistance.

8. *Shoulder Rotation* (Figures 13-37a, 13-37b)
Stand erect with fists clenched.
Rotate the arms in, hold, rotate the arms out, hold.
Repeat ten times, change arms.
Relax and repeat.
Hold 5-pound weights for more resistance.
For variation, extend palms flat and rotate as in sculling action.

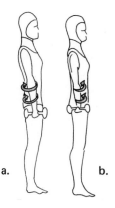

Figures 13-37a, 13-37b. Shoulder Rotation

9. *Arm Circles* (Figure 13-38)
Begin with arms at side, standing erect.
Make small circles forward with hands.
Increase size of circle.
Continue by decreasing size of circle.
Repeat five times.
Relax and repeat.
Use small weights to increase resistance.

10. *Straight-Arm Flexes* (Figures 13-39a, 13-39b)
Stand erect.
Hold 5- to 10-pound barbells, arms straight out in front of body.

Figure 13-38. Arm Circles

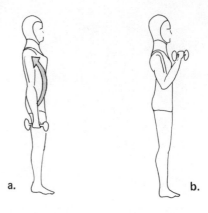

Figures 13-40a, 13-40b. Arm Flexion

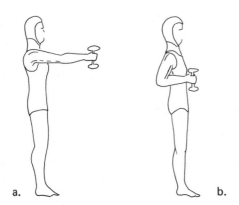

Figures 13-39a, 13-39b. Straight-Arm Flexes

Flex elbows, go back as far as possible.
Extend elbows and repeat.
Relax and repeat.
For variation, rotate arms, palms up, holding weights.
Repeat exercise as above.

11. *Arm Flexion* (Figures 13-40a, 13-40b)
Start in standing erect position.
Hold 5- to 10-pound weight.
Arm at side, elbow extended.
Flex elbow, bringing hand toward shoulder.
Return to straight-arm position.
Repeat ten times.

Relax and repeat.
Change arms.

12. *Bar Dips* (Figure 13-41)
Use overhand grip on bars.
Jump up to flexed-elbow position.
Keep head back, point toes, arch feet.
Press back on heels.
Dip body down, press back up.
Repeat five to ten times.
Relax and repeat.

Figure 13-41. Bar Dips

Exercises for the Neck

1. *Bridging* (Figure 13-42)
Lie on floor, arms at side, knees flexed, heels in close to the buttocks.
Pressing on the arms, on the back of the head, and on the feet, lift the

Figure 13-42. Bridging

hips and shoulders off the floor.
Relax and repeat.
2. *Neck Twister* (Figure 13-43)
Stand erect, hands on neck.
Turn head right and press backward.
Turn head back to starting position.
Turn head left and press backward, return to normal.
Press neck hard against hands.
Relax and repeat.

Figure 13-43. Neck Twister

3. *Chest Lifter* (Figure 13-44)
Lie on back with arms extended sideward to shoulder level, palms down.
Lift chest with extension of upper spine and by pressing down with the neck muscles.
Hold, return.
Relax and repeat.

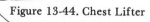

Figure 13-44. Chest Lifter

4. *Head Roll* (Figures 13-45a, 13-45b)
Stand erect.
Press head forward and hold.
Press head back and hold.
Roll head to right side, hold, then to left side and hold.
Roll head to right 90 degrees, roll head to left.
Circle head all the way around from left to right.
Repeat entire exercise 5 times.
Relax and repeat.

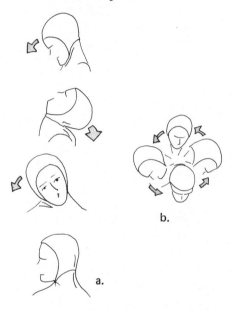

Figures 13-45a, 13-45b. Head Roll

Exercises for the Hips and Legs

1. *Forward Lunges—Prone Position* (Figures 13-46)
Hands on floor, arms supporting body.
Legs extended straight out.
Quickly bring left foot between hands. Extend left leg as right leg is brought between the hands.
Continue at a rapid pace, 20 to 30 seconds.
Relax and repeat.

Figure 13-46. Forward Lunges—Prone Position

2. *Sitting Knee Flexes* (Figures 13-47a, 13-47b, 13-47c)

Sitting position, hands behind head, elbows back.

Legs flat and together.

Draw both knees up toward chest as far as possible. Clasp with arms and pull the legs closer to the chest, feet flat on floor, trying to keep legs and back in same position.

Stretch arms above head.

Relax and repeat.

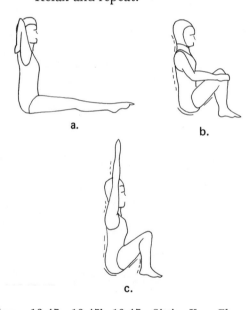

Figures 13-47a, 13-47b, 13-47c. Sitting Knee Flexes

3. *Kicker* (Figure 13-48)

Standing erect position.

Right hand extended straight forward.

Kick the right hand with the left foot. Keep both leg and arm straight, lock knee.

Figure 13-48. Kicker

Alternate hands and legs.

Point toes, arch foot.

Hold at top of kick.

Relax and repeat.

4. *One-Leg Pike* (Figures 13-49a, 13-49b)

Standing erect position, hands on hips.

One knee raised forward, then to the side, forward again, and back to the original position.

Repeat with other leg.

Hold 90-degree angle as each leg is raised.

Point toe and arch foot as leg is raised.

Repeat ten times with each leg.

Relax and repeat.

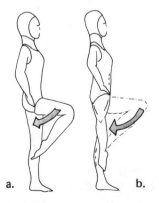

Figure 13-49a, 13-49b. One-Leg Pike

5. *Hurdle* (Figure 13-50)
Sitting position, trunk erect, left leg extended in front, right leg flexed at a right angle from the hip.
Flex trunk over and downward on the left knee (do not bounce).
Pull the head as close as possible to the knee.
Hands extend out toward foot.
Repeat to other side.
Relax and repeat.

Figure 13-50. Hurdle

6. *Step Forward* (Figure 13-51)
Standing erect position, one leg flexed and placed on a chair.
Lean forward, touch top of chair with hands.
Return to standing erect position and repeat, using the other leg.
Relax and repeat.

Figure 13-51. Step Forward

7. *Fencers' Lunge—Standing Position* (Figure 13-52)
Standing erect position.
Left foot is lunged sideward.

Figure 13-52. Fencers' Lunge—Standing Position

Right leg is extended and right hand above head.
Return to normal position.
Relax and repeat.

8. *Knee Bends* (Figure 13-53)
Standing erect position.
Flex hips and knees to bring body downward.
Upper trunk remains straight, hands in front for balance.
Slowly return to starting erect position.
Relax and repeat.
Half-knee bends can be done until full bends can be executed.

Figure 13-53. Knee Bends

9. *Thigh Stretches* (Figures 13-54a, 13-54b)
Start from a squatting position, fingers grasping toes.
Keep feet flat on floor and hold toes, extend the knees, pike forward.

a. b.

Figures 13-54a, 13-54b. Thigh Stretches

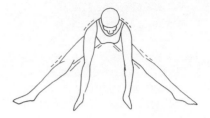

Figure 13-56. Side Straddle

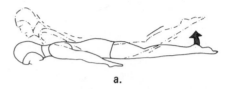

a.

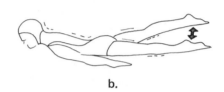

b.

Figures 13-57a, 13-57b. Reverse Leg Raises.

Hold 6 seconds before returning to starting squat position.
Relax and repeat.

10. *Back Roll* (Figure 13-55)
Lie on back, arms at side.
Bring trunk backward and upward, with the weight resting on the shoulders, and carry both legs overhead until they are at right angles to trunk.
Move legs up off floor, hold, drop.
Repeat five times.
Relax and repeat.

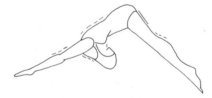

Figure 13-55. Back Roll

11. *Side Straddle* (Figure 13-56)
Start from a squatting position, weight evenly distributed on hands and feet.
Thrust the legs out sideways in a stride position.
Jump back to starting squat position.
Relax and repeat.

12. *Reverse Leg Raises* (Figures 13-57a, 13-57b)
Lie face down, arms at side, palms down.

Raise both legs behind body, spread them apart, bring together, and lower.
Relax and repeat.
Place 5-pound sandbags on each ankle for more resistance.

13. *Side Leg Swings* (Figure 13-58)
Standing erect position.
Swing right leg sideways five to ten times.
Switch and swing left leg sideways five to ten times.
Relax and repeat.

14. *Front and Back Leg Swings* (Figure 13-59)
Same as side leg swings except that the leg swings forward and backward.
Arch on the back swing and hold.
Relax and repeat.
Using ankle weights on Exercise 13 and 14 will increase resistance.

15. *Step Up* (Figure 13-60)
Start in standing erect position.

Figure 13-58. Side Leg Swings

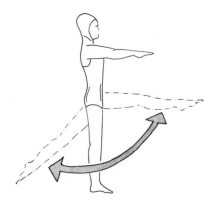

Figure 13-59. Front and Back Leg Swings

Figure 13-60. Step Up

Step up on low chair or stairs, right leg up, left leg up.
Step down one leg at a time.
Continue as fast as possible.
Repeat 10 times.
Relax and repeat.

16. *Knee Hugs* (Figure 13-61)
Standing erect position.
Draw left leg to chest, grasp knee, tuck as tightly as possible, point toes, arch foot.
Relax and repeat with right leg.

Figure 13-61. Knee Hugs

17.. *Toe Points* (Figures 13-62a, 13-62b)
Standing erect position.
Roll up on the toes, hold 5 seconds.
Roll back down on feet.
Repeat five to ten times.
Relax and repeat.

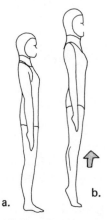

Figures 13-62a, 13-62b. Toe Points

18. *Ankle Rotation* (Figures 13-63a, 13-63b)

Standing erect position, feet flat on the floor.

Rotate right foot outward, hold, rotate inward, hold.

Repeat with left foot.

Repeat five to ten times with each foot.

Relax and repeat.

Point toes and arch foot as rotation occurs.

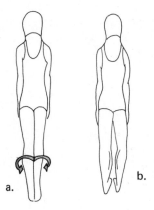

Figures 13-63a, 13-63b. Ankle Rotation

19. *Russian Sailor Dance* (Figure 13-64)

Start from squatting position, with arms out in front for balance.

Extend right leg forward, hold, return to squat position.

Repeat with left leg.

Increase speed of leg switch.

Point toe and arch foot during foward kick.

Repeat ten times.

Relax and repeat.

Figure 13-64. Russian Sailor Dance

20. *Splits—from Kneel* (Figure 13-65)

Start in kneeling position.

Place right leg forward, stretch as far forward as possible.

Repeat with left leg.

Change legs five to ten times.

Relax and repeat.

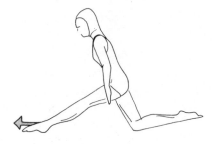

Figure 13-65. Splits—from Kneel

Exercises Specific for Endurance

1. *Jogging*

Jog a quarter of a mile, then rest 2 minutes and repeat run.

Increase the distance of the run, as conditioning takes place or decrease the time it takes to do the run.

Decrease the rest interval after three to four weeks of running.

2. *Jumping Jacks*

Standing erect position.

Jump to a position with feet apart and arms stretched above head.

Return to starting erect position.

Repeat fifteen to twenty times.

Rest 2 minutes.

Repeat.

3. *Running in Place*

Run as fast as possible in place for 3 minutes.

Rest 30 seconds.

Repeat two times.

Rest 2 minutes.

Repeat entire set.

4. *Running Up and Down Stairs*

Run up a set of stairs and walk back down.

Repeat ten to fifteen times.

Recovery will take place on the walking section.

5. *Jumping Rope*
   Jump rope 1 to 2 minutes continuously.
   Rest 30 seconds.
   Repeat two times.
   Rest 2 minutes.
   Repeat entire set.

CONCLUSION

It must be noted that the exercises listed in this chapter may have more than one function. For example, squat-thrusts are beneficial for endurance conditioning as well as for arm, shoulder, and chest strength. Using a variety of these exercises throughout the entire competitive season will enhance any synchronized swimming program. The swimmer should be strongly encouraged to continue her dry-land program every week. Strength and flexibility can only be increased in a consistent exercise program. The coach should keep regular charts on the progress of each of her swimmers. Station circuits can be set up with six to eight stations involving fourteen to sixteen varied exercises. A program of this type can accommodate from one to any number of swimmers within a short period of time (see diagram on p. 108).

Sample Workout for Stations

R=repeats

Station One

Exercises	Sets and Repeats
Sit-ups with a twist (can add weights if desired)	3X20[2]R
Chin lifts	5X10 R
Push-ups	4X10 R
Swan	5X10 R

Station Two

Back flings	5X10 R
Running up bleachers, walking down	Repeat 5 times (Rest 30 seconds between each repeat)
V-sits	5X5 R

Station Three

Running in place	3X1 minutes (Rest 30 seconds between each repeat) Rest 2 minutes Repeat twice
Static chin-ups	3X5 R
Slow bent-knee doubles	2X8 R

Station Four

Jumping rope	3X2 minutes (Rest 30 seconds between each repeat)
Nutcracker	5X5 R
Crisscross	5X8 R

Station Five

Knee hug	10X10 R
Back flings	5X10 R
Inward-outward leg rotation	10X10 R
Straight-arm flexes (with weights)	10X5 R
Arm flexion (with weights)	10X5 R

Station Six

Chest lifter	10X5 R
Squat-thrust—with push-up	5X5 R
Side splits	10X5 R
Back bend	5X5 R
Stick body	5X5 R

Any combination of exercises can be used, depending upon the need of the swimmers. A well-planned station workout can be a tremendous time-saver. Once the swimmers have been through this type of circuit training, the coach could then work on figures or routines in the pool with one group while another group is going through the station drills.

---

[2]The first number indicates the number of repetitions; the second one indicates the number of repeats or the length of time one must continue each repetition.

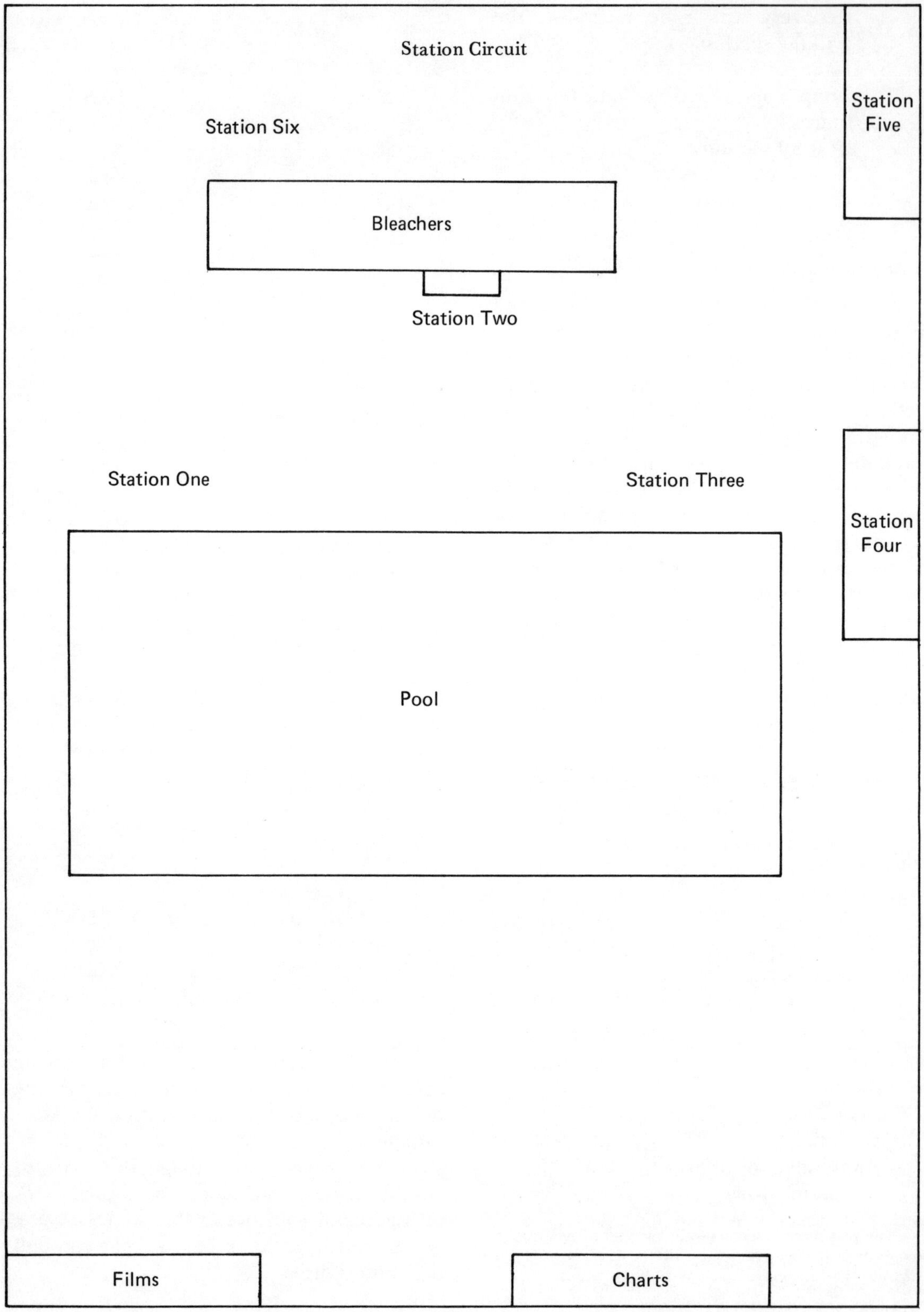

Station Circuit

Station Six

Station Five

Bleachers

Station Two

Station One

Station Three

Station Four

Pool

Films

Charts

Chapter 14

POOL CONDITIONING FOR THE SYNCHRONIZED SWIMMER

Pool conditioning in synchronized swimming is vital to any well-rounded program. As mentioned in the chapter on dry-land exercises, some major concepts must be kept in mind when designing the training program. There are numerous methods and techniques available to the coach and synchronized swimmer that can be used to enhance the general physical fitness level of the performer. Many training concepts used by the competitive swimmer can also be adapted for synchronized swimming. An in-depth study of competitive swimming would benefit the coach of any synchronized swimming team or club.

The following sections should provide a basis for any water training program. The swimmer ought to be in good physical condition before the training begins. It is necessary for the coach to explain the reasons for continuing the conditioning throughout the entire competitive season. Any training program should be set up on an individual basis; factors such as the mental and emotional capabilities of the swimmer will determine the amount of work the individual can handle. Daily activities, age, growth, and physical development levels will also affect the type of training loads each swimmer can manage. The coach must carefully assess each individual's potential and then plan a program accordingly.

INTERVAL TRAINING

The same basic principles of interval training for dry-land exercises can be applied to water conditioning. In addition, two other factors should be considered.

1. The mechanical principles applied to swimming, such as resistance, propulsion, and buoyancy (see Chapter 1).
2. The mechanics of stroke execution (see Chapter 3). Without sound swimming skills and efficient propulsion techniques the swimmer will become exhausted very rapidly.

Following are methods of interval training that should be used during the synchronized swimming season.

PRESEASON TRAINING

1. *Fartlek or Speedplay*—involves free or relaxed swimming interspersed with fast sprints or hard laps. A variety of strokes should be used so that the synchronized swimmer develops proper techniques for all strokes. The coach can make stroke corrections during the slow and relaxed swimming phase of this method of training. Examples of fartlek or speedplay training are as follows:
   a. Easy swimming for 3 to 5

minutes with a fast swim of 100 yards timed.

b. Easy swimming for 400 yards, followed by a paced (50 percent effort) 200-yard individual medley (50 fly, 50 back, 50 breast, 50 free).

c. Easy swimming for 5 minutes, with a modified freestyle or breaststroke head up, followed by a hard 50-yard sprint.

d. Combine any two of the three above and repeat three to four times.

Many combinations can be developed for this method of training. The coach must vary the program so that workouts are interesting.

2. *Over-Distance*—involves the use of distance with pace swimming. Both over-distance and fartlek training will develop general endurance and cardiovascular efficiency. The synchronized swimmer needs to develop endurance early in the season to be able to handle the longer workouts needed for swimming routines.

Examples of over-distance training are as follows:

a. Freestyle easy swimming for 4X400 yards. Rest 3 minutes between each set.

b. Continuous easy swimming for 1600 yards.

c. Easy swimming for 2X800 yards, changing strokes every 200 yards.

d. Easy swimming for 4X200 yards and for variety a 50-yard sculling in between each 200-yard swim.

Any ballet-leg or sculling drill can be added between sets at the start and finish of a practice with figure work done in between.

MID-SEASON TRAINING

After the preseason conditioning a portion of the daily workout should be devoted to interval training. This should be done at least three times per week even during routine work for maximum conditioning.

Interval swimming involves controlled distance, speed, and repetitions with specified rest periods. A general rule for repeats for a synchronized swimmer would be to have the heartbeat brought up to 160 to 165 during the overloading part of the interval workout and sustain this rate. The recovery or rest periods between repeats should be gradually shortened.

1. *Repeat Methods*—Variety in repeats is important to establishing an interesting interval training program. The instructor or coach should plan her workouts ahead of time and post them on a board. Prior to the start of any season it would be useful to explain to the swimmers the pool patterns and methods of repeats that will be used during the season.

Examples of repeat methods are as follows:

a. Sets of straight repeats: Repeat a certain distance with a consistent rest. Establish a time limit for repeats.

b. Split repeats:
   1) Increasing—each repeat is faster.
   2) Decreasing—each repeat is slower.

c. Distance repeats:
   1) Increasing—distance is increased with each set.
   2) Decreasing—distance is decreased with each set.

d. Locomotor repeats—the swimmer swims one length fast and rests, then swims two lengths fast and rests, then swims three lengths fast and rests, then four lengths fast and rests, then five lengths fast and rests, then six lengths fast and rests, then swims six lengths slow and rests, then five lengths slow and rests, then four lengths slow and rests, then three lengths slow and rests, then two lengths slow and rests, then one length slow and finishes.

e. Ladder repeats—three to five repeats with a short rest in between repeats. Long rest, then another set with increasing number of repeats. Reach ten repeats, then start back down, decreasing the number of repeats.

f. Slow, pace, sprint repeats— three slow repeats, three pace (50 percent effort) repeats, three sprint repeats (90 percent effort). Interchange slow, pace, and sprint repeats. Time these repeats to check swimmer's effort.

g. Combination repeats—alternate distance with interspersed rest intervals, or sprint repeats with distance repeats. The rest interval can be changed at various sprint or distance repeats for variety. Be sure to check the pulse rate increase and pulse rate recovery at various times for efficient use of work loads.

2. Examples of interval training are as follows:

Objective: To strengthen strokes and start long interval repeats.

a. 1X400 I.M. (fly, back, breast, free)
2 minutes rest

b. 2X200 freestyle
1 minute rest between sets

c. 5X75 (vary strokes) pull one length, kick one length, swim one length
30 seconds rest between each set

d. 4X100 (vary strokes) pull two, kick two

30 seconds rest between each set

e. 10X50 increasing repeats (each successive repeat is faster)
20 seconds rest between each set

f. 1X100 easy warm-down

3. Any variation of the above can be used. Sculling repeats, timed for speed, can also be interspersed between sets. Long intervals with controlled rest periods should be used for at least 50 percent of the mid-season workouts. Pool time and routine work will determine the amount of time devoted to long interval work but some portion of the weeks' practices should be set aside for regular repeats.

Objective: To start overloading with shorter intervals.

a. 3X200 I.M.
5X100 alternate fly and free on 1:45-2:00 minutes
5X100 free on 1:30-1:45 minutes
5X100 alternate back and free on 1:45-2:00 minutes
5X100 free on 1:30-1:45 minutes
5X100 alternate breast and free on 1:45-2:00 minutes
5X100 free on 1:30-1:45 minutes
1X200 sculling for warm-down

b. 1X500 alternate 100 free and 100 ballet-legs, single
5X200 free on 3:00 minutes
5X100 (free, back, or breast) on 1:45-1:50 minutes
10X50 free on 1:00 minute

c. 1X200 ballet-legs, double
2X200 kicking any stroke; time the 200 and set a certain time to do the repeats
5X100 free, increasing the speed on each 25 of every 100
10X50 free on 1:00 minute
2X100 alternate ballet-legs at moderate speed for warm-down

4. Many variations should be used with the above workouts. The main objective is to have the swimmer do the repeat within a specified time. For example, after the swimmer can handle 10X50 free on 1:00 minute, then time each 50-yard swim and have her hold a certain time.

   a. 2X50 free—38 seconds each; rest 15 seconds

   b. 2X50 free—35 seconds each; rest 15 seconds

   c. 2X50 free—all-out sprint; rest 15 seconds

The pulse should be checked at various times to see if the heart rate is between 160 to 165 beats per minute. It must be remembered that each swimmer's ability to do short intervals will vary. The coach should determine the capability of her swimmer and then set up individual goals for repeats. The use of a pace clock will aid the repeat workouts.

When trying to peak swimmers for competition the use of interval training is a necessity. Although most of the workouts later in the season will be devoted to figure and routine development, the coach should plan for timed repeats with controlled stress swims as often as possible.

DRILL VARIATIONS FOR SYNCHRONIZED SWIMMERS

Kicking and Treading Water Drills

Purpose: To increase leg strength and efficiency in kicking and treading water.

1. Flutter-kick races—may be done with kickboards, arms extended, or hands clasped behind the back and head out of the water.

2. Over and under kicking—kick one length at the surface and then one length under the water. Start with widths until strength and endurance are developed. Vary the kicks.

3. Partner kicks—have two swimmers face each other with a kickboard between them. Holding on to the board, each swimmer will kick, trying to force the other person backward. Be sure to keep the arms straight and the kickboard on the surface.

4. Ten-ten kicking—stomach—the swimmer executes ten flutter kicks while lying on her side, bottom arm extended overhead. A good layout, side, must be maintained. The bottom arm then pulls toward the body as the swimmer rolls across her stomach to the other side. Execute ten more kicks and repeat. Scissors kicks can also be used.

5. Ten-ten kicking—back—same as above except that the swimmer rolls across her back when changing from one side to the other.

6. Roll kicking—start in a layout, front, position with the hands in front of the body and complete ten kicks. Roll to the right side and do ten kicks, roll on to the back and do ten kicks, until the desired distance is completed. Kicks can be varied when changing body positions. The swimmer must continue to kick as she is changing position in the water.

7. Head-up kicking—the head and shoulders are held as high as possible, the lower back is arched, and the hands are clasped behind the back near the hips. Any number of flutter kicks or breaststroke kicks can be done in this manner. Head-up kicking in a vertical position with the hands above the head can also be used.

8. Vertical kicking—swimmer is vertical in the water, feet toward the bottom of the pool, hands completely extended over the head, executing a strong flutter kick. Do 30 seconds, rest, and repeat three to four times.

9. Dolphin-kick series.
   a. Dolphin kick—on one side for a specified number of kicks and then roll to the other side.
   b. Regular dolphin kicks—in layout, front, position, arms extended in front of the body. The head can be held slightly up to put more stress on the kick.
   c. Dolphin kick—on the back.
   d. Dolphin bobs—the swimmer sinks to the bottom of the pool and does dolphin kicks up to the surface. Repeat ten times.
10. Eggbeater kick series.
   a. Breaststroke bobs—the swimmer sinks to the bottom of the pool and does the breaststroke kick up to the surface. Repeat ten times.
   b. Stationary eggbeater—the swimmer's hands are above the head or slightly above the head when holding a 5-pound weight. Do 3 minutes of eggbeater, rest, then repeat three to four times.
   c. Eggbeater bobs—same as breaststroke bobs. Have the swimmers hold weights or weighted bricks for more resistance.
   d. Moving eggbeater—the swimmers do lengths of the eggbeater kick. This should be done both forward and backward for teaching propulsion in this kick.

The coach should constantly encourage the swimmers to use good body positions, back extended and head up, when practicing the eggbeater kick.

11. Combination kicking—any of the above drills can be used with combinations of kicks. For example, the swimmer could combine five flutter kicks with two breaststroke kicks, or two scissors kicks, five flutter kicks, and two breaststroke kicks. These kicks should be done while changing body positions and while swimming lengths.

Kicking drills are vital for the development of good synchronized swimmers. Without efficient use of kicks, fast-moving routines and quick changes of direction in routines will be difficult to obtain. The instructor or coach should include some of these drills in her repeat workouts. It is important for swimmers to be timed on lengths and they must be made to repeat faster and faster times. Otherwise, the lengths of these drills will be of little value.

Pulling and Arm-Stroke Drills

Purpose: To increase arm strength and efficiency in the propulsive parts of arm strokes in swimming.

1. Swim distances or repeats using arm strokes only. During the interval training periods, repeats of regular stroke pulls can be very beneficial. The use of a variety of pulls will be useful for the synchronized swimmer. The butterfly arm pull should not be avoided because it can develop arm, shoulder, and back strength very quickly. The use of pull-buoys and hand paddles will help with this drill.
2. Static line pulls.
   a. Using about 10 feet of surgical tubing or a similar material, tie one end around the swimmer's legs and have a partner hold on to the other end. The swimmer in the water begins to do the arm pull of any stroke while the partner on deck pulls on the tubing. The more the tubing stretches, the more efficient the stroke. The modified strokes for synchronized swimming could be used in this drill.
3. Breaststroke pull drills.
   a. Do short breaststroke pulls with the hands in front of the body.

The elbows must remain extended and all the action comes from the wrists. (This is a good lead up for pike down-front.)

b. Underwater pulls—do lengths of underwater swimming using just the breaststroke pull. Start with widths until strength is developed.

c. Breaststroke pullouts underwater—one breaststroke pull is executed. The elbows are drawn quickly in to the sides of the body. Then the hands and arms push the water along directly back toward the feet until the arms are straight along the sides near the hips. To recover, draw the arms up along the sides of the body until they are stretched out completely in front of the head. Repeat pullout, either on the surface or underwater. No kicking should be used. A glide should be held at the beginning. This drill is excellent for developing arm and shoulder strength.

d. Breaststroke pulls with head up.

4. Freestyle and backstroke pull drills.

a. One-arm pulls—pull one length of freestyle sculling with one hand in front of the body and pulling with the other hand. Pull the entire length with one arm. In the backstroke, pull with one arm while sculling at the hip with the other. Rolling slightly on the side helps develop a longer pull for both strokes.

b. Head up, one-arm pull—swimming freestyle, repeat the above drill while keeping the head up. Scull with the non-pulling arm in front of the body.

c. Hold a kickboard in one hand and stroke with the other arm in freestyle.

d. Combination pulls—combining pulls will assist in developing the stroking needed for routines. For example, do a series of breaststroke pulls, then change to sidestrokes, then to back crawls.

The swimmer should concentrate entirely on the pull when doing these drills. Timing lengths of pulls will encourage the swimmer to work to capacity.

Breath Control Drills

Purpose: To increase lung capacity and cardiorespiratory endurance.

1. Over and unders—one length on the surface and one length underwater. Time the length on the surface to ensure the swimmer is not moving too slowly. For large numbers of swimmers, organize over and unders so that there are swimmers on the surface at all times. Use all six lanes of the pool and divide the group into six groups of five to eight swimmers in each lane. Repeat four to six times with no rest between lengths.

2. Bobbing—submerge underwater slowly, blowing air out of the mouth; surface, take another breath, and submerge again.

3. Swim two lengths of front crawl without breathing.

Sculling Drills

Purpose: To increase sculling efficiency and arm strength.

1. Lengths of all of the various sculls (see Chapter 4)—the swimmer should be encouraged to vary the speed of the sculls while practicing.

2. Sculling and movement progression combinations—sculling drills can be combined with many of the movement progressions used in figures. For example, the swimmer does a headfirst scull—layout, back—with hands at the hips for one-half

length, then does a pike drop-back to a feetfirst scull—layout, front—with hands overhead and sculls for the remaining half length. Many combinations can be developed to build good transitions from position to position.

3. Support sculling, vertical position—the swimmer assumes a vertical position with the feet toward the bottom of the pool. The swimmer executes the support scull action until her feet touch the bottom of the pool. This drill can be done in the bent-knee variant and crane positions.

4. Support sculling bobs—the swimmer assumes an inverted vertical position with the head toward the bottom of the pool. She support sculls up as high as possible and holds the height for a few seconds. Then she drops toward the bottom and support sculls up as high as possible once again. Ten to fifteen bobs should be done in the vertical position. This drill can be done in the bent-knee variant and crane positions.

Ballet-Leg Drills

Purpose: To increase strength and control in the ballet-leg movements.

1. Two lengths of bent-knee variant, layout, back, position. Foot of the bent knee at or near the surface of the water. After this position is correct have the swimmer lift the foot 2 to 3 inches higher, so that the leg from the knee to the toe is parallel to the surface of the water. Both headfirst and feetfirst sculls should be used.

2. Alternate ballet-legs both headfirst and feetfirst.
   Variation: Cross right leg over left leg and press against the vertical leg. Scull both headfirst and feetfirst in this position. Change the vertical leg.

3. Ballet-legs, double, drills.
   a. Double bent-knee variant, layout, back, position—scull feetfirst and headfirst in this position.
   b. Lift both feet 2 or 3 inches higher so that the leg from the knee to the toe is parallel to the surface of the water. Scull both headfirst and feetfirst.
   c. Extend the knees from the previous position so that the legs are at a 45-degree angle to the surface of the water. Scull both feetfirst and headfirst in this position.
   d. Fully extend into a ballet-legs, double, position. Scull both headfirst and feetfirst in this position.

4. Flamingo position, sculling both feetfirst and headfirst.

5. Straight-leg ballet-leg changes—change legs without going through the bent-knee variant position. Scull both feetfirst and headfirst in this drill.

Ballet-leg drills are extremely important for routine and figure work. More overload can be placed upon the swimmer by doing timed repeats with any of the above drills.

Figure Coordination Drills

Purpose: to develop transitions within figures, support sculling, and basic body positions and to encourage original hybrids.

1. Pike down-front to vertical lift. Drop one leg into a crane position. Lift the horizontal leg to an inverted vertical position and submerge.

2. Tuck on back, surface, to inverted tuck position. Lift to an inverted bent-knee variant, complete a 180-degree spin. Lift to an inverted vertical position and submerge.

3. Establish a crane position. Lift the horizontal leg to a 45-degree angle above the surface of the water.

Hold, return to a crane position. Repeat, changing the vertical leg.

4. Breaststroke into a pike down-front. Complete a vertical lift to a side split position. Hold, slowly drop the legs to a front and back split. Lift both legs simultaneously to an inverted vertical position and submerge.

5. Execute a pike drop-back, scull up to an inverted vertical position. Drop one leg as the feet break the surface of the water (crane position). Pull the horizontal leg into a bent-knee variant position. Submerge with an albatross spin.

6. Support scull—be sure there is no pause between the following movements. Inverted tuck, inverted bent-knee variant, crane position (left leg vertical), change crane position (right leg vertical), back to an inverted bent-knee variant, end in an inverted tuck position. Repeat several times.

Any of the above drills may be combined with closed or open spins for variety. Swimmers can be very creative in developing these kinds of drills. A microphone can be used so that the coach can give counts while large groups of swimmers practice together.

TEACHING AND TRAINING AIDS

The following teaching and training devices can be very useful in adding variety to daily workouts. The coach or instructor should become familiar with these devices and use them to aid her swimmers.

1. Pace clock—a large clock with a minute and second hand. A pace clock can be very helpful in permitting swimmers to work at their own level. For example:
   a. Start each swimmer on 5-second intervals, swim 50 yards, and repeat another 50 on the minute.
   b. On intervals of 1:45, a 5X100-yard swim. The swimmer will learn to pace the 100-yard swim so she has a 15- to 20-second rest. Each swimmer watches the pace clock for her start.

2. Stopwatch—there are numerous brands of stopwatches but a split timer will be more beneficial for timing many swimmers at the same time. On a split timer the main hand runs continuously and the second hand or split hand appears when the button is depressed.
   To operate a stopwatch:
   a. Hold the watch between the thumb and index finger.
   b. Use the bone part of the index finger for starting and stopping the watch. Do not time with the thumb.
   c. Hold the watch up in front of you and take any slack out of the crown.
   d. Read the time with the hand of the watch at twelve o'clock. This will give a better angle for reading.
   e. If the minute hand is in the black, read the black number. If the minute hand is in the red, read the red number.

3. Hand paddles—used to create more resistance and to assist the swimmer in feeling the propulsive phases of pulls or sculls. It consists of a flat plastic paddle with an elastic band for the hand.

4. Kickboards—used to correct kicks or strengthen legs.

5. Pull-buoys—used to maintain streamlined body positions or for pulling or sculling drills. The buoys consist of two circular styrofoam cylinders tied together with plastic

rope. Pull-buoys can be used to practice the pike down-front movement progression or supported inverted positions such as the inverted vertical and inverted tuck positions. The buoys are placed between the ankles for support.

6. Swim fins—used to develop the power phases of kicks. Swim fins are also good for teaching dolphin kicks.

7. Mirror—placed in the water to help the swimmer see where she is putting her hands in support sculling or figure work.

8. Skin-diving mask—very useful to swimmers in observing their underwater arm movements. Can be used by partners for figure analysis.

9. Goggles—used to protect the swimmer's eyes from irritation due to prolonged sessions in the water.

10. Underwater sound equipment—very effective training aids during figure work or workouts. The instructor or coach can hook up an underwater microphone for immediate corrections or group figure work.

11. Films—super 8 films can be advantageous for routine and figure analysis. An underwater housing can be obtained for any super 8 camera so that underwater shots can be taken.

12. Video tape—for instant replay, a video tape system can be used.

13. Stop-action photos—can be used to show routine formation and positions within patterns.

14. Loop films—any super 8 films can be made into a loop film for continuous showing.

POOL PATTERNS

Pool patterns must be set up early in the season to enable the daily workouts to run efficiently. It would be advisable to have several practice sessions using a variety of pool patterns to demonstrate how they can be used. Following are patterns that could be used by any instructor or coach.

X	=	Swimmer
– – –	=	Path swimmer is moving
→	=	Direction
G1,G2,etc.	=	Group designation

1. One-lane circles—eight to ten swimmers swim up the lane and down the gap (space between lanes) in a circle pattern. For safety reasons, it is wise to swim the crowded lanes in the same direction down the gap.

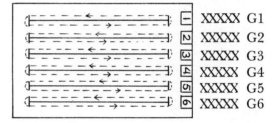

2. Two-lane circles—up lane one, down lane two, up lane three, down lane four, up lane five, down lane six. Continuous swims are best in circles.

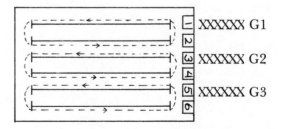

3. V's—split the pool into three V's. Make sure each swimmer swims toward the gap between the lanes to make a turn. This is particularly efficient for 50-yard repeats.

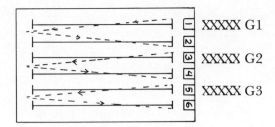

4. M's and W's—half of the swimmers are lined up on the deck, single file, at one end of the pool while the other half are lined up at the other end of the pool. Group One starts swimming in a "follow the leader" fashion up lane one, down between lanes two and three, up lane four, and down between lanes five and six. When the last person in Group One starts on her second lap, the first person in Group Two starts. Group Two will trace the exact same pattern as Group One.

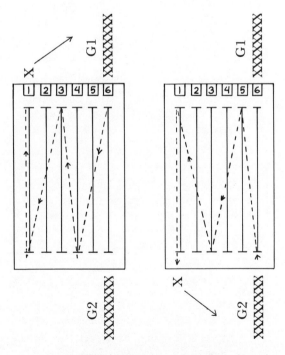

This pattern of swimming is good for doing a continuous 100-yard workout. Both groups can keep on moving, resting long enough to get out of the pool and return to the starting point. Ballet-leg or sculling drills done using this pattern will give practice in changing directions.

5. Snakes—any number of swimmers may be involved. The swimmers begin one at a time, 5 seconds apart, and follow in a line. The pattern moves up one lane, down the second lane, up the third lane, and continues until all six lengths are completed.

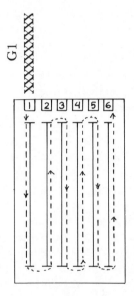

For a large number of swimmers a group can be started on each end of the pool. As one group finishes the first length of the snake, the other group starts.

6. Split 75's—two groups start—one on lane one and one on lane six. Begin on the same side of the pool in a "follow the leader" fashion. Each group swims three complete lengths, getting out of the water at the opposite ends of the pool and walking back to the starting point. Each swimmer should be instructed

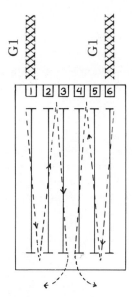

to swim on a lane and turn between the lanes.

The coach can position herself between the two finish lanes making individual corrections as the swimmers get out of the water. This drill can be useful for one-pull, one-kick, one-swim drills.

7. L's—Group One in this formation swims 50 yards and Group Two swims two widths. As Group One passes, at the beginning of their 50 yards, Group Two starts and must swim over and back before Group One returns.

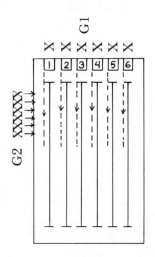

8. Double L's—four groups can be organized to swim a box formation. This is the same as the L drill, only with a group on each end and side of the pool. The coach can time Group One and Group Three on their 50-yard swim. It must be remembered that Group Two and Group Four must finish their two widths before the 50-yards are completed by Group One or Group Three. The coach can run these repeats as fast or as slow as she wishes. After a certain number of 50's, Group One and Group Three exchange positions with Group Two and Group Four. The swimmers doing widths could swim one underwater for variety. For larger groups more heats can be added behind the groups.

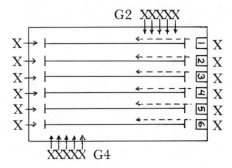

9. Widths—half the group swims across the pool while the other half watches and makes helpful corrections. Continuously rotate groups, doing as many widths as desired.

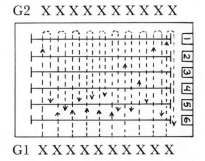

10. Waves—line up as many heats as desired and swim one length of the pool, starting the groups 5 seconds apart.

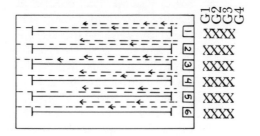

11. Z's—swimmers start on the side of the pool, one at a time in line formation, swimming one width, then one length on a diagonal, and finishing with another width. This

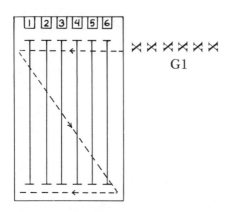

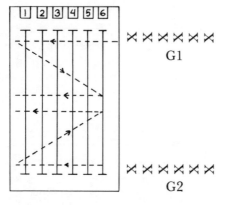

formation would be useful for ballet-leg and sculling drills to teach change of direction. For example: the first width, do ballet-legs,

double, headfirst direction; diagonal, feetfirst ballet-legs, double; last width, ballet-legs, double, headfirst direction.

To accommodate more swimmers divide the pool in half with two Z's moving at the same time.

12. R's—this formation is similar to the Z principle and can be useful for teaching direction changes. The coach should make it very clear which lanes the swimmers move on. The fastest swimmers should go first.

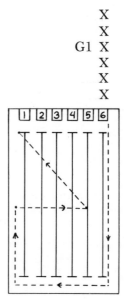

13. Zigzags—Group One starts on lane six, sculls over to lane one, back to

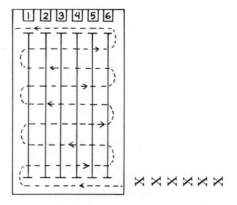

lane six, back to lane one, and so on, until one entire length of the pool is completed. The swimmer must watch for other swimmers and must move down the pool on every change of direction. A ballet-leg or stroke-change drill can be used effectively with this pattern.

14. Eights—the swimmers swim, using modified strokes, doing ballet-legs, and/or sculling in a figure-eight formation in the pool. The swimmers must watch for other swimmers as they cross the center of the eight. This is a good drill for making swimmers aware of pattern changes and circle formations, and watching for their teammates. Use lane numbers to guide the swimmers in this drill.

Many variations for the above pool patterns can be used by the coach or instructor. Variety in any drill program will

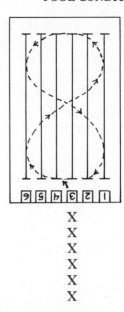

keep the swimmers alert and interested in what they are doing.

SYNCHRONIZED SWIMMING WORKOUT SHEET
(Water Conditioning)

Name_____ Day_____ Month _____ Year _____

Workout	Sets	Repeats	Repeat Times	Yardage

Type of Training:
Strengths:
Weaknesses:
Coach's Comments:

(Dry-Land Exercises)

Workout	Sets	Repeats	Repeat Times	Type of Exercise

Type of Training:
Strengths:
Weaknesses:
Coach's Comments:

Chapter 15

SYNCHRONIZED SWIMMING ORGANIZATIONS

Once the swimmer has mastered the fundamental skills of synchronized swimming she can organize and combine these skills in a routine or composition. This routine can be used for A.A.U. competition, I.A.A.A. evaluation, or intercollegiate and interscholastic competition. The swimmer must be familiar with the objectives and methods of evaluation of the organization in which she wants to participate. The swimmer can then write her routine accordingly.

The purpose of this chapter is to present a general overview of the three major synchronized swimming organizations. The authors recommend writing to the specific organizations listed at the end of this chapter for further details.

A.A.U. SYNCHRONIZED SWIMMING COMPETITION

In 1940, David Clark Leach and Katherine Curtis drew up rules for duet and team competition in synchronized swimming. These rules provided a fairly objective method of evaluating routines in terms of execution, style (costuming, lighting effect, showmanship, manner of performance, effectiveness), composition, and accompaniment. The A.A.U. recognized these rules in 1945 and one year later the first national duet and team synchronized swimming competition was held in Chicago. Solo competition was added in 1950. Today, an A.A.U. competitor may enter figure competition and routine competition in solo, duet, and/or team events.

CLASSES OF COMPETITION

Within the framework of the A.A.U. rules, the following classes of competition are provided to accommodate swimmers of varying ability: senior national, junior national, senior association, junior association, junior olympics, age group, and novice. Each class of competition has both figure competition and routine competition in solo, duet, and team events. Every swimmer who competes in a routine event must compete in figure competition, as her score determines, in part, her final routine score.

FIGURE COMPETITION

The A.A.U. rule book lists approximately 135 recognized figures. Each figure has a degree of difficulty ranging from 1.1 (the easiest to execute) to 2.4. Only those figures listed in the rule book may be performed in figure competition.

Each class of competition lists specific figures that must be performed. In the most advanced levels of competition (senior national, junior national, and senior association) a specific set of six figures is drawn, prior to the meet, from a group of six possible sets. In the less advanced levels (junior association, junior olympics, age group, and novice) the same three figures are performed in every meet and in addition the swimmer selects two optional figures of her choice.

The swimmer performs each figure before a panel of from five to seven judges. Each judge awards a score ranging from 0 to 10 (10 being the best). The highs and lows are canceled and the remaining scores are added. The sum of the scores is then multiplied by the degree of difficulty of the figure. This procedure is used for each figure performed. The individual scores for each figure are then added together and divided by ten. This number is the individual's figure score.

ROUTINE COMPETITION

Routine competition includes solo, duet, and team (four to eight swimmers) events. There are only three major routine requirements: deck work must be 20 seconds or less; solos and duets must be 4 minutes or less and teams, 5 minutes or less; and every routine must include five recognized figures that are performed simultaneously by all members of the routine.

Every routine is performed before a panel of five to seven judges. The judges give the routines two scores: one for execution and one for content. These scores range from 0 to 10 (10 being the best). The first score to be flashed is the execution score. The highs and lows are canceled and the remaining scores are added. The sum of the scores is then multiplied by the routine's degree of difficulty for the five recognized figures (not to exceed 1.8). This number becomes the execution award for the routine.

The second score to be flashed by the judges is the content score. The highs and lows are canceled and the remaining scores are added. This number becomes the content award for the routine.

The total score is then determined by adding the execution award, the content award, and the figure award. The figure award for a solo is the score received in figure competition. The figure award for a duet or team is the sum of the figure awards of each member divided by the number of members.[1]

THE INTERNATIONAL ACADEMY OF AQUATIC ART

In 1955 the International Academy of Aquatic Art was organized to promote swimming as a performing art rather than a competitive sport. The objectives of this organization, as stated in its articles of incorporation, are:

"To recognize and explore the potential of the aquatic medium for truly artistic self-expression and interpretation.

"To establish an academic environment conducive to the full development of aquatic art forms.

"To interest the people of the world in participating in the development of aquatic art."[2]

INTERNATIONAL FESTIVALS

Each year, usually in the spring, an International Aquatic Art Festival is held with participation open to all men and women who are I.A.A.A. members. In order to prevent too lengthy a festival, the number of compositions is limited (usually to sixty). Entries are accepted in the order they are received. A club may enter three compositions if these are 5 minutes or less. If the composition runs over 5 minutes, but not over 10 minutes, it is counted as two compositions. If the composition runs over 10 minutes (maximum, 15 minutes) it is counted as three compositions. An individual member may enter only one composition, either a solo or a duet with another individual member. Each solo must be 5 minutes or less in length.

---

[1] Printed with permission from A.A.U. Synchronized Swimming Rule Book. Copyright 1974 by the Amateur Athletic Union of the United States, Inc.

[2] Printed with permission from the bylaws of the I.A.A.A.

There are seven classes of compositions that may be presented: solo, duet, trio, group (four or more swimmers), duet mixed (man and woman), trio mixed (any proportion of men and women), and group mixed (four or more swimmers with any proportion of men and women). The compositions usually are arranged in five presentation sessions with twelve compositions per session. To add interest to the festival each presentation session is arranged so that a variety of classes are included. It is recommended that any composition that has not received a rating above an "A" from the critics be placed in the first presentation session.

Critics

The compositions are performed before an audience, which includes a panel of five critics. These critics are "flexible-minded people of mature judgment and approved by the I.A.A.A. Board of Control. Flexible-minded people of mature judgment are fundamentally people with an innate or trained sense of values."[3] The only requirements for the compositions are that they be in good taste, of relatively short duration, with a major portion of the composition performed in the water.

Each critic gives a rating that represents his evaluation of the composition. The critic must consider the total composition instead of attempting to analyze or assign specific weight to component parts of the composition. The critic then uses his personal experience and judgment to arrive at a rating.

Immediately following a presentation session, an evaluation session is held. This session is open to all interested people attending the festival and it is here that comments are given by the critics and ratings are announced.

Ratings

Four ratings may be given at the International Aquatic Art Festival: "IAAA," "AAA," "AA," and "A." The highest rating in aquatic art ("IAAA") is given only to those compositions that the critics feel make a definite contribution to the development of aquatic art. These compositions create and sustain a strong emotional impact throughout the entire performance (requiring a high degree of proficiency and sensitivity in the areas of choreography and performance).

INTERCOLLEGIATE AND INTERSCHOLASTIC COMPETITION

In 1974, the Intercollegiate Synchronized Swimming Coaches Association was formed and established national guidelines for competitive synchronized swimming. Until this time intercollegiate competition had been taking place in various sections of the country on an individual basis.

CLASSES OF COMPETITION

The following classes of competition are provided to accommodate swimmers of varying ability: senior, junior, and novice. Each class of competition has both figure competition and routine in solo, duet, trio, and team events. (The novice class does not have solo events.) A competitor need not compete in figure competition to compete in routine competition.

FIGURE COMPETITION

The A.A.U. rules are used for figure competition. Each class of competition lists specific figures that must be performed. In the senior division, six groups of six figures are rotated on a yearly basis.

In the junior division, three groups of four figures are rotated. In addition to these four, two optional figures are performed. These optionals must be a 1.9 degree of difficulty or below. For novice

---

[3] Printed with permission from *Aquatic Artist*, Vol. XIX, p. 7. Published by the International Academy of Aquatic Art, Cedar Rapids, Iowa.

competition the figures are determined by the meet director.

ROUTINE COMPETITION

Routine competition includes solo, duet, trio, and team (four to eight swimmers) events. These routines are completely free routines with no figure requirement. It is recommended that no routine be longer than 5 minutes with a 30-second deck limit.

Every routine is performed before a panel of five to seven judges. The judges give the routines two scores: one for execution and one for content. These scores range from 0 to 10 (10 being the best). The first score to be flashed is the execution score. The highs and lows are canceled and the remaining scores are added. This number becomes the execution award for the routine. The second score to be flashed by the judges is the content score. The highs and lows are canceled and the remaining scores are added. This number becomes the content award for the routine. The total score for the routine is then determined by adding the execution score and the content score.

For further details write to:

A.A.U. Synchronized Swimming Rule Book
Book Order
Amateur Athletic Union of the United States
3400 West 86th Street
Indianapolis, Indiana 46268

I.A.A.A. Rules
The International Academy of Aquatic Art
206 Iowa Theatre Building
Cedar Rapids, Iowa 52401

Intercollegiate Rules (NAGWS)
National Association for Girls and Women in Sport
1201 16th Street, N.W.
Washington, D.C. 20036

Chapter 16

ROUTINE DEVELOPMENT

Upon mastery of the fundamental skills of synchronized swimming, the swimmer can organize these skills in a routine or composition. The way in which these skills are combined will be dependent upon the type of organization in which the swimmer wishes to participate (Chapter 15).

Composing a routine can be a very rewarding experience if the swimmer follows a basic outline of routine development. For this reason the following outline is offered.

1. *Selection of Music*
   a. The music should fit the skill level of the swimmers. A classical selection that has rapid musical changes ("Russian Sailor Dance") is much more difficult to swim to than a selection that has a solid musical beat ("Puppet on a String").
   b. A good selection should have changes in rhythm and mood.
   c. The length of the selection must be considered. If the routine will be used for competition, the selection must conform to standards.
   d. The swimmers should be involved in the selection of the music so they can begin to plan their interpretation (Spanish music would suggest Spanish movements).
   e. The selection should appeal to all members in the routine because it will be played over and over many times.
   f. Instrumental music is easier to count than vocal selections.
   g. Some good contemporary orchestrations have been made by Arthur Fiedler and the Boston Pops Orchestra, Richard Bonynge and the London Symphony Orchestra, Henry Mancini, 101 Strings, the Moody Blues, Leonard Bernstein, Fritz Reiner, Percy Faith, and Broadway Sound Tracks.
   h. Good sources for classical music are such composers as Anton Dvořak, Richard Strauss, Joseph Herold, Peter Tchaikovsky, Ludwig van Beethoven, Johannes Brahms, Aaron Copland, Reinhold Glière, Jacques Offenbach, and Wolfgang Mozart.
2. *Analyzation of Music*
   a. Graphically analyzing the music will give the swimmers something tangible to work with. One way to do this is to put a mark down on paper for every beat and then use symbols to indicate variations.

4/4 /—¢—/≤ ≥/—ss—/———/

/—···—/—F——/———/—|•|——/

b. Many variations can be used to graph out music but it is important that all swimmers understand the symbols being used. Following are some symbol suggestions:

/ = phrase change in music

/ / / / = each vertical line represents a beat

¢ = change

< = build up in music

> = fast to slow change

S = sustained counts

• • • = staccato beats

F = fast section

≡ = sharp notes—symbol crash or drum beats

/•/ = count change

≤ = end of routine or section

c. Mark the basic underlying beats and then count out those beats many times while listening to the selection. Once familiar with the selection, go back and mark the changes and variations.

d. Use the first beat of the measure as the primary count and begin most figures and strokes on that beat.

3. *Content of Routine*

a. Select figures, hybrids, and strokes that *all* swimmers can do well.

b. Determine the number of beats it takes to complete figures and hybrids and see where they fit into the music. Be sure there are enough beats for transitions into and out of these figures.

c. Be sure to use the music effectively. On fast-moving sections, slow, sustained figures would be inappropriate. On music build-ups, movements such as spins and lifts should be used.

4. *Routine Structure*

a. Choreography should begin and end with the music.

b. Each swimmer should be given a number before trying to develop pool patterns.

c. Pattern development.

1) Use the entire pool if possible.

2) Vary the patterns and plan for swimming transitions into and out of each formation.

3) Each swimmer should know her position in relation to the other swimmers in the pattern.

4) Use lane markings to help position the swimmers.

5) Use both surface and underwater formation changes.

d. Diagram the pattern changes and have the swimmers walk through them on the deck before trying them in the water.

5. *Preliminary Land Drills*

a. Each swimmer should have a copy of the routine when land drilling.

b. Count out every movement on land.

c. Have one or two swimmers try the movements in the water.

d. A count tape recording can be made so the swimmers learn the correct counts quickly.

6. *Water Work*

a. Try figures and stroke sections separately.

b. Divide the routine into sections and try each part with the music. Do not be afraid to reconstruct sections if the original ideas do not work well.

c. Patterns develop slowly. Sections may have to be performed in the water a number of times before a definite pattern is established.

7. *Land Drills*
   a. Special land drill sessions should be scheduled so that swimmers can learn the routine.
   b. The swimmers should count the routine out loud at every land drill workout.
8. *Routine Revisions*
   a. If sections of the routine do not work out the swimmers should go back to Step 3 and revise accordingly.
   b. Each swimmer should sit out a few times to watch the routine.
   c. The use of video tapes will help when making revisions.
   d. Be open for suggestions from other swimmers and coaches.
9. *Helpful Hints*
   a. Continue to land drill the routine after it is learned.

   b. Don't be afraid to repeat moves in your routine. Repetition can add to the development of a theme.
   c. It helps to have an idea or theme that you wish to express in your routine, but don't let it bind you and stifle creativity.
   d. Be sure to project and make a conscious effort to continuously change your focus.
   e. Don't be afraid to experiment with new and different patterns.
   f. Much hard work and practice is necessary for the successful development of a routine.

Choreographing routines is a very complex task. Although this chapter provides a basic outline for swimmers to use when writing routines, the authors suggest checking dance references for a detailed analysis of the elements of choreography.

Chapter 17

HOSTING COMPETITIVE SYNCHRONIZED SWIMMING MEETS

Because of the sudden growth and interest in competitive sports for women, it is quite likely that many public school teachers, college instructors, and aquatic specialists will be called upon to host competitive synchronized swimming meets. The purpose of this chapter is to summarize the A.A.U. and intercollegiate rules and provide a workable format to follow for hosting competitive synchronized swimming meets. The authors recommend writing for the specific rules for greater detail.

PRELIMINARY INFORMATION

At least four weeks prior to the meet send out an announcement to include the following:

1. Date, time, and location of meet
2. Type of meet and rules to be used
3. Classes of competition
4. Eligibility
5. Order of events
6. Type of awards
7. Point system for team trophies
8. Entry forms
9. Entry fee and deadline
10. Practice times
11. Coaches' meeting and awards banquet
12. Needed officials
13. Name, address, and phone of meet director
14. Map of area with parking information

15. List of accommodations
16. Transportation available
17. List of restaurants
18. Diagram and explanation of pool to include:
    a. Pool dimensions: Depth, water level below deck, position of diving board and starting blocks if immobile, ladders
    b. Markings on the bottom and side
    c. Type of lighting
    d. Position of audience
    e. Open space for entrance and exit
    f. Type of sound equipment: Tape recorders, turntables, underwater speakers
    g. Information for competitors on accompaniment: All competitors must include the following identification on their accompaniment: name, school or club, desired side, band, and basic speed. No tape should contain more than one accompaniment per side and its beginning on the tape should be clearly identified by a suitable leader.
    h. Alternate facilities, if available

It is recommended that competition, other than Nationals, be held in a pool having an area of at least 25X35 feet not less than 9 feet in depth. For National

131

competition there must be an area of 25X40 feet. None of the competitive area shall be less than 3 feet deep and water must be of sufficient clarity for the bottom of the pool to be clearly visible and the water temperature shall be no less than 78 degrees Fahrenheit.[1]

FIGURE COMPETITION

PREMEET PROCEDURES

1. Check all figure sheets for the correct signatures, the correct number of groups, and the correct degrees of difficulty.
2. Check eligibility and entry fees.
3. Draw for order of contestants and prepare sheets to post and distribute to coaches. The competitors should be randomly grouped in flights of six.
4. Provide a list of officials for the referee.
5. Publicize the meet.
6. Arrange for a coaches' meeting to answer questions concerning the meet and to determine judges.

FIGURE MEET OFFICIALS

1. Meet manager
2. Referee
3. Vice-referee
4. Clerk of course
5. Figure judges (preferably nine for each panel)
6. Announcers (two)
7. Scorers (three or more)
8. Runners (two)
9. Typist

Meet Manager

Shall assume responsibility for sending out preliminary information and premeet procedures.

[1] Printed with permission from A.A.U. Synchronized Swimming Rule Book. Copyright 1974 by the Amateur Athletic Union of the United States, Inc.

Referee

Shall have full jurisdiction over the meet, shall enforce all rules and decisions governing the meet, and shall decide all questions concerning the conduct of the meet.

Referee and Vice-Referee

1. Shall position themselves in the center of the panel of judges.
2. When the contestant is ready, they shall signal by blowing a whistle.
3. When the contestant completes the figure, they shall signal for the judges' awards by blowing a whistle.
4. After the judges' awards have been recorded, they shall instruct the scoring table of infractions and penalties, and advise the competitor of the decision.

Referee's Penalties

1. One point penalty for deviating 90 degrees more or less from a listed twist or spin.
2. One point penalty for adding a twist or spin to a listed figure.
3. One point penalty for taking a swimming stroke prior to the execution of a figure.
4. One point penalty for failing to complete the required sequence of a figure.
5. If a competitor makes a balk or false start or does not complete a figure, she is allowed a second attempt and the referee instructs the scorers to reduce the score for the individual figure by one third.
6. If a competitor executes a listed figure other than the one announced, the referee shall rule it failed and not call for awards.

Clerk of Course

1. Shall obtain the order of draw and make sure that all competitors in a given flight are ready.

2. Shall notify each flight of the order of performance and the sequence of figures to be performed.

Figure Judges

Shall judge the competitor from the sound of the referee's whistle until the completion of the figure. Upon the sound of the referee's whistle for awards, the judge shall visibly flash the score.

Methods of Grading

1. Design—5 points
   a. Horizontal body position
   b. Vertical body position
   c. Circle
   d. Back pike position
   e. Front pike position
   f. Tuck position
   g. Ballet-leg position
   h. Flamingo position
   i. Crane position
   j. Split position
   k. Knight position

2. Control—5 points
   a. Full body extension
   b. Smooth transitions within the figure, constant speed of action
   c. Compactness of front and back tucks and back pikes
   d. Confident, seemingly effortless execution
   e. Proper elevation of the body in relation to the surface of the water
   f. Performance of figure in a relatively stationary position

Figure Scoring

Excellent ☐ 9-10
Design—Near perfection of body position
Control—Effortless, near perfection

Good ☐ 7-8½
Design—Good body position
Control—Above satisfactory

Satisfactory ☐ 5-6½
Design—Average
Control—Average

Unsatisfactory ☐ 3-4½
Design—Unsteady body positions
Control—Weak

Deficient ☐ ½-2½
Design—Figure recognizable, major deficiencies
Control—Very poor

Failed ☐ 0
Unrecognizable as listed figure or figure performed other than listed

Announcers

1. Shall announce the number of the competitor and the figure to be performed.
2. Shall announce the judges' awards in sequence.

Scorers (See Sample Figure Score Sheet, page 134.)

1. Record the individual awards, each time in the same consecutive order, on a score sheet.
2. If nine judges are used, cancel the two highest and two lowest awards. If five or seven judges are used, cancel only the one highest and one lowest award. If three judges are used, there shall be no cancellation.
3. Add the remaining awards and multiply the sum by the degree of difficulty of the figure.
4. Follow the same procedure for each of the figures.
5. Add the scores for the individual figures for each competitor, individually, and divide by ten. This quotient is the individual's figure score.
6. If either five or three judges are used, multiply the individual's figure score by 5/3. If nine or seven judges are used, omit this step.

SAMPLE FIGURE SCORE SHEET

NAME: _JEANNE BROWN_

REPRESENTING: _WASHINGTON HIGH SCHOOL_

CITY & STATE: _LINCOLN, IOWA_

TYPE MEET: _HIGH SCHOOL_

WHERE HELD: _JEFFERSON, IOWA_

DATE: _5/13/75_

SOLO	X	ORDER
		7
DUET		PLACE
TEAM		15

	FIGURE NO.	FIGURE NAME	JUDGES' AWARDS									TOTAL MINUS HIS-LOS	DEG. OF DIFF.	SCORE POINTS
			1	2	3	4	5	6	7	8	9			
1	112	EIFFEL WALK	5.5	5.0	6.0	5.5	5.5	6.0	6.0	5.5	5.5	28	1.7	47.60
2	201	ALBATROSS	5.5	5.5	6.0	5.5	6.0	6.0	5.5	6.0	6.5	29	1.9	55.10
3	403	ELEVATOR	5.0	6.0	6.5	6.0	6.0	6.5	6.0	6.0	6.0	30	2.0	60.00
4	315	SOMERSUB, BACK PIKE SOMERSAULT	6.0	7.0	6.5	6.5	6.0	6.5	5.5	6.0	6.5	31.5	1.6	50.40
5	309a	PORPOISE, SPINNING, 360	6.5	6.5	6.0	6.5	7.0	6.5	6.0	6.5	7.0	32.5	1.9	61.75
6	202	CASTLE	6.5	7.0	6.5	7.0	6.5	6.5	6.5	6.5	6.5	32.5	2.2	71.50

DESCRIPTION OF PENALTIES:

OUT OF SEQUENCE ON #112

REFEREE: _SALLY DILLON_

SCORER: _JOYCE GREENFIELD_

SUB-TOTAL:	34.635
PENALTIES:	1.000
TOTAL:	33.635

SIG. OF CONTESTANT: _Jeanne Brown_   AGE: _18_

Runners

Shall deliver score sheets to the appropriate tables as the meet progresses.

Typist

Shall immediately type results of the meet and distribute them to the coaches.

ROUTINE COMPETITION

PREMEET PROCEDURES

1. Check all routine sheets for the correct signatures, the correct number of groups, and the correct degrees of difficulty. For A.A.U. routines there must be five required figures that are listed and per-

formed as described in the A.A.U. rules. All members of the routine must perform these figures simultaneously. These figures listed on the sheet represent the degree of difficulty multiple for the routine. For purposes of computation the sum of the five difficulty multiples may not exceed 9.0 (although a higher difficulty sum may be shown on the sheet). Of the five figures, no more than two figures may be listed from the same number group (100-400), and no more than one figure of the same number may be listed. For intercollegiate competition, the routines are free and the competitors need not list figures or degrees of difficulty.

2. Check eligibility and entry fees.
3. Draw for order of routines and prepare sheets to post and distribute to coaches. For A.A.U. competition, the suggested order of events is solo, duet, and team. For intercollegiate competition it is solo, duet, trio, and team competition.
4. Provide a list of officials for the referee.
5. Arrange for a coaches' meeting to answer questions concerning the meet and to determine judges.

ROUTINE MEET OFFICIALS

1. Meet manager
2. Referee
3. Vice-referee (A.A.U. meet only)
4. Clerk of course
5. Routine judges (seven)
6. Announcer
7. Scorers (three or more)
8. Timers (three) (A.A.U. meet only)
9. Readers (two) (A.A.U. meet only)
10. Sound center manager
11. Underwater sound monitor
12. Runners (three)
13. Recorders (seven) (intercollegiate only)
14. Typist

Meet Manager

Shall assume responsibility for sending out preliminary information and premeet procedures.

Referee

1. Shall have full jurisdiction over the meet, shall enforce all rules and decisions governing the meet, and shall decide all questions concerning the conduct of the meet.
2. When the contestants are ready, he shall signal by blowing a whistle.
3. When the contestants are finished, he shall signal for the judges' awards by blowing a whistle.

Referee and Vice-Referee (not applicable to intercollegiate)

1. Shall check the performance of the contestants against their submitted sheets.
2. Shall confer on any questions of infraction of rules against the competitor, and after the judges' awards have been recorded the referee shall instruct the scoring table of the decision and record penalties while the vice-referee instructs the competitors and coach of the infractions.

Referee's Penalties (applicable to A.A.U. competition)

1. One point penalty for one or more competitors performing the routine with a change in the order of listed figures.
2. One point penalty for one or more competitors failing to perform a recognized required figure.
3. One point penalty for one or more competitors failing to begin and/or finish with the accompaniment.
4. One point penalty for exceeding the following time limits for routines: 4 minutes for solo and duets, and 5 minutes for team competition.

5. One point penalty for exceeding the twenty-second deck limit.
6. One point penalty if one or more competitors interrupt the routine during deck movements and make a new start.
7. One point penalty for failing to end the routine in the water.
8. One point penalty if any competitor fails to perform a listed twist or spin.
9. One point penalty for deliberately walking on the bottom (maximum of two points given per routine).
10. One point penalty for failing to complete a required sequence of a figure that is listed as a required figure.
11. When a competitor omits a listed routine figure the penalties are as follows:
    solo—five points per omission
    duet—three points per omission
    team—one point per omission
12. Failure to complete the routine after entering the water results in disqualification.

Clerk of Course

Shall obtain the order of draw and make sure that all competitors are ready.

Routine Judges

Shall judge the routines from the sound of the referee's whistle until completion of the routine. Each judge records both the execution and content grades on a sheet of paper and hands it to the runner. Upon the sound of the referee's whistle for awards, the judge shall visibly flash the execution award. Upon a second signal, the content scores are flashed. Judges shall award grades from 0 to 10, with 1/10-point variations on both execution and content scores.

Execution Scoring for A.A.U. and Intercollegiate Competition

Excellent	9-10
Good	7-8.9
Satisfactory	5-6.9
Unsatisfactory	3-4.9
Deficient	0.1-2.9
Failed	0

Content Scoring for A.A.U. and Intercollegiate Competition

1. Synchronization—one with the other and with the accompaniment

Solo	Duet,Trio,Team
1	4

2. Construction

a. Creative action	Solo	Duet,Trio,Team
	2	1
b. Fluidity	2	1
c. Difficulty	4	3
d. Variety	1	1

Announcer

1. Shall announce the number of the routine. Title is announced in intercollegiate competition.
2. When the scores are flashed, shall announce the awards in sequence for both execution and content.
3. After the scores have been given, the names and affiliations of the swimmers may be announced.

Scorers

Routine scoring for A.A.U. Competition (see Sample Routine Score Sheet, page 138).

Execution Score

1. Record the individual awards, each time in the same consecutive order, on a score sheet.
2. Cancel the two highest and two lowest awards if seven judges are used. If five judges are used, cancel only the one highest and one lowest award. If three judges are used, there shall be no cancellation.

3. Add the remaining awards and multiply the sum by the average degree of difficulty multiples divided by five and carried to the fourth decimal, not to exceed 1.8.

In team competition, one-half point shall be added to the total score for each additional competitor over four on a team. A team may have as many as eight members.

4. This procedure gives the score for execution of the routine.

Content Score

1. Record the individual awards, each time in the same consecutive order, on a score sheet.
2. Cancel the two highest and two lowest awards if seven judges are used. If five judges are used, cancel only the one highest and one lowest award. If three judges are used, there shall be no cancellation.
3. Add the remaining awards for content. This constitutes the content score. There shall be no multiplication of the content score.

Total Routine Score

The total score shall be the sum of the scores for figures for each swimmer (divided by the number of swimmers), execution of the routine, content of the routine, and the team bonus points if any, less the referee's penalties.

Routine Scoring for Intercollegiate Competition

Execution Score

1. Record the individual awards, each time in the same consecutive order, on a score sheet.
2. Cancel the two highest and two lowest awards if seven judges are used. If five judges are used cancel only the one highest and one lowest award. If three judges are used, there shall be no cancellation.

3. This procedure gives the score for execution.

Content Score

Use the same procedure as above to get the content score.

Total Routine Score

The total routine score shall be the sum of the scores for execution of the routine and content of the routine.

Timers (not applicable to intercollegiate competition)

The timers shall check the overall time of the routine as well as that of the deck movements. The deck and total routine times shall be recorded on the Routine Score Sheet. If the time on two watches agrees, that time shall be the official time. Should the times of all three watches differ, the intermediate time shall be the official time. When the time of either the overall routine or the deck movements is in excess of the limit a timer shall so inform the referee.

Readers (not applicable to intercollegiate competition)

Shall perform duties as assigned by the referee. These usually include reading the required figures prior to their performance in the routine.

Sound Center Manager

1. Shall be responsible for the reproduction of sound from recorded discs and/or tapes for the accompaniment for each routine.
2. Shall obtain the order of draw, and arrange the discs and/or tapes in proper sequence for presentation.

Underwater Sound Monitor

Shall test for sound underwater

SAMPLE ROUTINE SCORE SHEET

TEAM NAME: *DOLPHINS*

REPRESENTING: *WASHINGTON HIGH SCHOOL*

TITLE: *LONDON FOLLIES*

TYPE MEET: *HIGH SCHOOL*

WHERE HELD: *JEFFERSON, IOWA*   DATE: *5/13/75*

ORDER	
7	5
PLACE	
3	2

COMP. FIGURE NO.	SKELETAL FORM OF ROUTINE: LIST EXACTLY IN ORDER OF PERFORMANCE:	DEG. OF DIFF.	TEAM CONTESTANTS' NAMES:	FIGURE SCORES
108	CATALARC	1.9	1. JEANNE BROWN	25.170
302	BARRACUDA	1.8	2. MAY SCHMIDT	27.120
421	WALKOVER, BACK	1.7	3. SALLY ANDERSON	26.851
309	HERON	1.7	4. JULIE SMITH	26.442
201	ALBATROSS	1.9	5. DIXIE JONES	28.664
			6. RUTH SWEET	26.571
			7. LINDA MEYERS	26.430
			8. ROSIE BELL	26.680
			ALT. MARY NELSON	25.526

DESCRIPTION OF PENALTIES:

SIGN. OF COACH: *Ruth Larson*

TOTAL DIFFICULTY MULTIPLES:	9.0	DEGREE OF DIFFICULTY FOR SCORERS
DIVIDED BY FIVE:	1.8	TO COMPUTE: ___1.8___

Judges' No.	1	2	3	4	5	6	7	Total	Score
Exec. Award	4.1	4.3	4.2	4.2	4.1	4.0	4.0	12.40	22.32
Content Award	4.2	4.2	4.1	4.2	4.1	4.3	4.2	12.70	12.70

Judges' No.	1	2	3	4	5	6	7	Total	Score
Exec. Award	4.2	4.3	4.3	4.4	4.3	4.3	4.3	12.90	23.22
Content Award	4.3	4.3	4.3	4.4	4.6	4.3	4.3	12.90	12.90

DECK TIME: *10:30*	POINTS:	35.02
	PENALTIES:	
OVERALL TIME:	BONUS PTS:	
	SUB-TOTAL:	35.020
	FIGURE SCORE:	26.616
	PRELIMINARY TOTAL:	61.636

DECK TIME: *10:30*	POINTS:	36.12
	PENALTIES:	
OVERALL TIME: *4:55.10*	BONUS PTS:	
	SUB-TOTAL:	36.120
	FIGURE:	26.616
	FINAL TOTAL:	62.736

REFEREE: *SALLY DILLON*

SCORER: *JOYCE GREENFIELD*

REFEREE: *BETTY WOODS*

SCORER: *JANE MILLER*

during the accompaniment test, prior to every seventh routine.

Recorders (applicable to intercollegiate competition only)

Shall record the judges' comments concerning both the execution and content of each routine.

Runners

Shall deliver score forms as directed by the referee.

Typist

Shall immediately type results of the meet and distribute them to the coaches.

Chapter 18

YEARLY UNIT PLAN FOR TEACHING OR COACHING SYNCHRONIZED SWIMMING

Season from
September 1 through
August 10.

September

Week One
1. Tryouts for team.
   a. Swimming skills analyzed.
   b. Sculling analyzed.
   c. Figures for intermediate and advanced tryouts.
   d. Physical exams due.
2. Team meeting.
   a. Introduction of new team members and coaches.
   b. Review of team philosophy.
   c. Yearly goals.
   d. Review of training techniques.
   e. Standards and objectives for swimmers.
   f. Team input.
   g. Workouts scheduled.
   h. Introduction of coaches.
3. Meeting with parents.
   a. Introduction to coaches.
   b. Team philosophy and standards.
   c. Types of workouts that will be used.
   d. Financial obligations (important to be complete about cost of meets, shows, suits, and club dues).
   e. Responsibilities of parents (bake sales, ticket sales, driving to meets, scoring).
   f. Parents input and suggestions and any new ideas.
   g. Workout schedule. It is important to establish a good working relationship with parents early in the season. The head coach should make it clear that the coaching should be left up to the faculty and staff members who are trained in this area. Information given to the parents concerning the type of training program that will be used will provide a better understanding of the dedication needed by the swimmer.
4. Coaches meeting.
   a. Objectives.
      1) Seasonal objectives.
      2) Age-group training variations.
      3) Meet objectives.
      4) Meet schedule.
      5) Monthly, weekly, and daily objectives.
   b. Practice assignments.
      1) Pool.
      2) Age-group.
   c. Further meetings set up.
   d. Practice procedures.
      1) Organization.
      2) Efficient use of time.

141

e. Techniques.
    1) Types of basics taught should be similar.
    2) Skill progressions.
    3) Movement progressions.
    4) Routine development.
    5) Dry-land conditioning.
    6) Water conditioning.
f. Policies.
    1) Swimmers.
    2) Parents.
    3) Coaches.
g. Needs.
    1) Attendance.
    2) Effort.
    3) Careful planning.
h. Equipment needed.
    1) Exercise weights.
    2) Training aids.
    3) Clocks.
5. Team picnic.

Weeks Two, Three, and Four

Objectives: To start dry-land conditioning, water-training drills, and introduce movement progressions.

1. Exercises.
   a. Should be varied and chosen from all categories (see Chapter 13).
   b. Rest intervals should be long.
   c. Equal distribution of strength, flexibility, and endurance should be chosen.
   d. Physical fitness testing (should be done early in month).
2. Workouts
   a. Over-distance swimming. Vary strokes. Make basic stroke corrections immediately. Have stroke clinics if needed.
   b. Kick drills.
   c. Pull drills.
   d. Sculling drills.
   e. Ballet-leg drills.
3. Movement progressions (this will vary according to the skill level of the swimmers). All basic body positions should be introduced on land

before starting movement progressions.
   a. *Ballet-leg*
       1. Ballet-leg, single.
       2. Ballet-leg, single, submarine.
       3. Side ballet-leg, submerged.
   b. *Tuck*
       1. Tub.
       2. Tuck on back, surface.
       3. Back tuck somersault.
       4. Front tuck somersault.
   c. *Pike*
       1. Pike drop-back.
       2. Back pike somersault.
       3. Pike down-front (use pull-buoys for practice).
   d. *Arch*
       1. Shark circle.
       2. Dolphin.
   e. *Rotational*
       1. Surface twist.
       Intermediate groups should review these sections of the progressions. Advanced groups should work figures related to these progressions.
4. Music selection. Time should be devoted to screening musical selections for possible use in routines. This month would also be good for introduction to choreography basics (see Chapter 16).
5. End-of-the-month review of each swimmer.
   a. Workout sheet of work accomplished by each swimmer should be analyzed by the head coach (see Chapter 14).
   b. Exercise chart should be analyzed to assess changes needed.

October

Week One

Objectives: To increase training loads in dry-land and water conditioning. To continue movement progressions and to start basic choreography of routines and count out music.

1. Exercises.
   a. Should be changed for variety, keeping an equal distribution of all areas of fitness conditioning.
   b. Rest intervals should be shortened by 20 percent.
   c. Load should be increased 25 percent.
2. Workouts.
   a. Fartlek or speedplay training should be introduced. Vary strokes.
   b. More stress put on kicking and pulling drills. Timed kicks and pulls.
   c. Breath-control drills should begin.
   d. Add variety in sculling drills.
   e. Continue ballet-leg drills.
   f. Begin figure-coordination drills for intermediate and advanced groups.
   g. Start modified stroke drills, combination kicking, and pulling.
   h. Do movement progressions learned last month with combination stroking.
3. Movement progressions.
   a. *Ballet-leg.*
      1) T position, surface.
      2) Ballet-legs, double.
      3) Ballet-legs, double, submarine.
   b. *Tuck*
      1) Inverted tuck (introduce support sculling at this point).
   c. *Pike*
      1) Front pike (continue introduction of support sculling with this progression).
      2) Front pike somersault.
   d. *Arch*
      1) Dolphin.
      2) Dolphin feetfirst.
      3) Front press bent knee.
4. Music selection and counting out beats.

Week Two

Objectives: To continue with previous week's schedule and to review support sculling.
1. Exercises are the same as the week before.
2. Workouts are the same as the week before (combine movement progressions in drills).
3. Support sculling.
   a. Land drills—introduce body positions.
   b. Feetfirst—vertical bobs with support sculling.
   c. Bent-knee variant position (feetfirst) with support sculling.
   d. Crane position (feetfirst) with support sculling. Stress the body positions and correct placement of the hands during these drills.
   e. Put swimmers against the wall with partners holding them in inverted vertical, crane, bent-knee variant, and tuck positions for practice.
4. Continue with music selection and counting out beats. Start stroking ideas with music in water.

Weeks Three and Four

Objectives: To increase work loads on exercises and pool training. To continue movement progressions.
1. Exercises.
   a. Continue with same exercises as set up during Week One.
   b. Add weights (5 pounds) where applicable.
2. Workouts.
   a. Continue Fartlek or speedplay.
   b. Add support sculling drills. Emphasize technique!
3. Movement progressions (combine movement progressions for practice).
   a. *Ballet-leg.*
      1) Crane.
      2) Ballet-leg, tip back.
      3) Ballet-leg, tip up.

4) Ballet-leg roll, single.
5) Ballet-legs roll, double.
  b. *Arch*
1) Dolphin feetfirst to bent-knee variant.
2) Dolphin feetfirst to vertical.
3) Dolphin feetfirst to crane.
4) Front press straight leg.
5) Arch to vertical.
  c. *Lifting and unrolling.*
1) Inverted tuck to vertical.
  d. *Transitional.*
1) Walk-out, front.
2) Walk-out, back.
4. Music analysis with figure and stroking ideas.
5. End-of-the-month review of each swimmer (same as last month).

November

Week One

Objectives: To start long interval training with exercises and pool work. To introduce rotational and lifting and unrolling movements. To start putting sections of the routine together.
1. Exercises.
  a. Change some of the flexibility exercises and add more strength and endurance to each station.
  b. Continue with weights.
  c. Start controlled repeats with timed rest intervals.
2. Workouts.
  a. Start long interval conditioning with timed repeats and timed rest intervals. Check pulse rate periodically to see if rate, at this period of conditioning, reaches between 120 to 140.
  b. Continue kicks and pulls with repeats.
  c. Add stress to ballet-leg drills.
  d. Continue breath-control drills (over and unders).
  e. Continue combination drills.
3. Movement progressions.
  a. *Rotational.*
1) Catalina reverse rotation.

2) Catalina rotation.
3) Swordalina rotation.
  b. *Lifting and Unrolling.*
1) Heron unroll.
2) Barracuda unroll.
  c. *Transitional.*
1) Front pike to crane.
2) Front pike to vertical.
3) Front pike to bent-knee variant.
4) Vertical to pike.
4. Routine writing.

Weeks Two and Three
1. Exercises.
  a. Continue with the same as Week One.
2. Workouts.
  a. Coninue with the same as Week One.
3. Movement progressions. Review as much as needed and go back and teach again if necessary. Combine progressions for practice.
  a. *Rotational.*
1) Pirouette rotation.
2) Gaviata rotation.
  b. *Lifting and Unrolling.*
1) Flamingo bent-knee unroll.
2) Flamingo unroll.
3) Aurora lift.
  c. *Transitional.*
1) Albatross roll.
2) Knight press back to bent-knee.
3) Crane to split.
4) Crane to vertical.
4. Routine work.

Week Four
1. Exercises.
  a. Continue with the same as Week One.
2. Workouts.
  a. Continue with the same as Week One. Add movement progression drills for practice.
3. Movement progressions. First introduce basic twists and spin actions.

Practice feetfirst until skill is acquired.

a. *Rotational.*
   1) Vertical half twist.
   2) Vertical full twist.
b. *Transitional.*
   1) Castle press back.
   2) Pirouette change.
   3) Side leg lift.
c. Work combinations of progressions learned thus far. For example: vertical half twist, to crane, to split.
d. Continue routine work, adding figures that have the movement progressions already learned.

4. Assign some figures and have an intersquad figure meet.
5. End-of-the-month review of each swimmer (same as last month).

December

Weeks One and Two

Objectives: To start short interval training for both land and water conditioning. To focus on twists and spins. To complete routines. To complete and review all movement progressions.

1. Exercises.
   a. Change flexibility exercises and repeat the ones done earlier in the season.
   b. Increase weights on resistance exercises.
   c. Continue with strength and endurance exercises.
   d. Shorten the number of exercises in each set but decrease the rest interval and decrease the time on repeats. Push for 75 percent overload.
2. Workouts.
   a. Start short interval training.
   b. Vary the types of repeats but decrease the rest interval and decrease the time on the repeats. Push for 75 percent overload. Continue to vary the strokes.

c. Continue kicking and pulling repeats.
d. Vary ballet-leg and modified stroke drills.
e. Add some games for interest.
f. Stress some figure coordination drills that use support sculling.
g. Focus on twists, spins, and open spins.

3. Movement progressions.
   a. *Rotational.*
      1) Bent-knee half twist.
      2) Bent-knee full twist.
      3) Crane twist.
      4) Bent-knee 180-degree spin.
      5) Bent-knee 360-degree spin.
      6) Vertical 180-degree spin.
      7) Vertical 360-degree spin.
   b. *Combination progressions.*
      1) Heron unroll to bent-knee 180-degree spin.
      2) Barracuda unroll to vertical 360-degree spin.
      3) Flamingo unroll to vertical full twist.
      4) Dolphin feetfirst to vertical to crane twist.

4. Routine work. Break routines into sections for workouts.
5. Continue working on required figures.

Weeks Three and Four

Objectives: To continue the objectives of Week One and Week Two. To review movement progressions with combinations. To continue routines and figure work.

1. Exercises.
   a. The same as Week One.
2. Workouts.
   a. The same as Week One. Encourage swimmers to sprint 95 percent on fast repeats.
3. Movement progressions.
   a. *Rotational.*
      1) Albatross 180-degree spin.
      2) Albatross 360-degree spin.
      3) Open spin.
   b. *Combination progressions.*

      1) Gaviata rotation to open spin.

      2) Barracuda unroll to open spin.

      3) Dolphin feetfirst to crane twist to open spin.

4. Routine work. Video tape or film routines for analysis.

5. Continue on required figures. Video tape or film figures for analysis.

6. End-of-the-month analysis of each swimmer.

January

Weeks One, Two, Three, and Four

1. During this month the conditioning program can be cut down slightly but the short interval training sessions on both exercise and pool work should be done at least twice a week. Stress overloading so that the heart rate will increase to 160 to 165 beats per minute on the heavy repeats.

2. Continue routine and figure work.

3. Some combination movement progression drills should be singled out for variety. Concentrate these drills on the swimmers' weak areas.

4. Film analysis will also be beneficial at this point.

5. End-of-the-month analysis of each swimmer should include teamwork, figure-score analysis from meets, and cooperative effort given by the swimmer to team spirit.

February

Weeks One, Two, Three, and Four

1. Change workouts by going back to some hard repeats of kicks and pulls. Continue ballet-leg drills and make sure swimmers are working to capacity. Time repeats of ballet-legs, double. Continue exercise program as much as possible.

2. Continue routine and figure work with film analysis.

3. For relief from competition stress, an intersquad water polo match or water volleyball game would add some variety.

4. End-of-the-month analysis of each swimmer.

March

Weeks One, Two, Three, and Four

1. For peaking swimmers for national, regional, or state competition, March would be a good time to reach maximum overloading in workouts. Devote some consistent time each week to the interval training program.

2. Detailed critiqueing of routines and figures is necessary at this point.

3. End-of-the-month analysis of each swimmer should include some suggestions on how to prepare mentally for peaking for competition.

4. Tapering should begin at least three weeks prior to national competition.

April

Weeks One, Two, Three, and Four

1. Tapering. Swimmers should cut their work load by 75 percent in interval training and concentrate largely on routines. The mistake many coaches make is to increase the work loads prior to a big meet. This keeps swimmers in a state of exhaustion and performance levels will drop.

2. Shorter workout periods should be stressed with long intervals for recovery.

3. General technique sessions should be done in figure and routine work.

4. Land-drill sessions should replace heavy exercise sessions. A certain amount of flexibility exercising should still be done.

5. A short vacation or rest should follow strenuous competition.

May, June, July, August
(depending on the type
of competition)

If there is another big competitive event in late summer the swimmers should be started back on a program similar to January, February, and March.

1. The coach should be very careful not to let the boredom factor set in and try to vary the workouts as much as possible.
2. Routines can be broken down again into sections for practice.
3. Short intervals will have to be worked gradually into the program again for pool and dry-land training sessions.
4. A review of some of the basics of movement progressions and support sculling would be useful to begin this period of training.

The preceding section deals primarily with a program that has a four- to five-day workout schedule per week. It might be noted that a sound conditioning program can be organized from the preceding material with less available pool time. Dry-land conditioning can be done on days when pool time is not available.

Variations of the program just explained can be adapted to any situation. The movement progressions may be taken at a slower pace, depending upon the skill level of the group. It is recommended that some of these progressions be taught prior to any formal figure instruction. They will provide a firm basis for later figure and routine work.

INDEX